"Here Am I"

"Here Am I"
Responding to God's Call

Sara Buswell

BAKER BOOK HOUSE
Grand Rapids, Michigan 49516

For Joshua, "God is salvation"
and
For Rachel, "God's ewe-lamb"

O my people, hear my teaching;
listen to the words of my mouth.
I will open my mouth in parables,
I will utter hidden things, things from of old—
what we have heard and known,
what our fathers have told us.
We will not hide them from their children;
we will tell the next generation
the praiseworthy deeds of the LORD,
his power, and the wonders he has done.

                              Psalm 78:1–4

Contents

Index of Hymns

Study Plan

1. Read the questions at the beginning of each lesson.

2. Read the Scripture passage(s) listed and be aware of the questions as you read. Allow time to think about words or phrases or incidents that are especially meaningful to you. Underline them in your Bible.

3. Formulate initial answer(s) to questions.

4. If possible, discuss answers with a friend or group.

5. Read the lesson commentary.

6. Revise answers, if necessary.

7. Apply your answers to your life as God directs.

1

Introductions
Searching for Self

Primary Scripture Readings

> Genesis 3:10; 22:1, 7: 27:18; 31:11; 46:2; 37:13
> Exodus 3:4
> 1 Samuel 3:2, 6, 8, 10, 16
> 2 Samuel 15:26
> Isaiah 6:8; 58:9
> Acts 9:10

Supplementary References

> Genesis 1:26–27
> Psalms 8, 103, 139
> Colossians 3:7 10

Questions for Study and Discussion

1. Choose two different English Bible translations and complete the chart on pages 14 and 15.

2. If the same term *Henani* is used in the original texts for each of the verses in the chart, what might explain the variations in English wording?

3. Consider the list of speakers in the chart. Is there anything about the personalities of these individuals that might suggest grouping them? What good and bad qualities do you remember about any of them? What do you expect to gain from this study?

4. What does the term *Here am I* convey to you? What would it (or its idiomatic equivalent) mean to you if you heard someone use it or said it yourself?

13

"Here am I"

VERSE	TRANSLATION 1 (_____)	TRANSLATION 2 (_____)	SPEAKER (to whom?)
Gen. 3:10	He answered, "I heard you in the garden, and I was afraid because I was naked; so I hid."		Adam (to Lord God)
Gen. 22:1			
Gen. 22:7			
Gen. 27:18			
Gen. 31:11			
Gen. 46:2			
Gen. 37:13			
Exod. 3:4			
1 Sam. 3:2, 6, 8, 10, 16			

VERSE	TRANSLATION 1 (_____)	TRANSLATION 2 (_____)	SPEAKER (to whom?)
2 Sam. 15:26			
Isa. 6:8			
Acts 9:10			
Isa. 58:9			

5. List some possible deterrents or obstacles that might keep a person from responding to God's call.

6. Who are you? Whether this is the first meeting of your group or a continuation of an ongoing class, or even if you are studying by yourself, try to compose a short paragraph of introduction (100 words or less) that captures your essential nature as an individual. How do you define or describe yourself?

T he Caterpillar and Alice looked at each other for some time in silence: at last the Caterpillar took the hookah out of its mouth, and addressed her in a languid, sleepy voice.

"Who are *you*?" said the Caterpillar.

This was not an encouraging opening for a conversation. Alice replied, rather shyly, "I—I hardly know, sir, just at present— at least I know who I *was* when I got up this morning, but I think I must have been changed several times since then."

"What do you mean by that?" said the Caterpillar sternly. "Explain yourself!"

"I can't explain *myself*, I'm afraid, sir," said Alice, "because I'm not myself, you see."

"I don't see," said the Caterpillar.

15

"I'm afraid I can't put it more clearly," Alice replied very politely, "for I can't understand it myself to begin with; and being so many different sizes in a day is very confusing."

"It isn't," said the Caterpillar.

"Well, perhaps you haven't found it so yet," said Alice, "but when you have to turn into a chrysalis—you will someday, you know—and then after that into a butterfly, I should think you'll feel it a little queer, won't you?"

"Not a bit," said the Caterpillar.

"Well, your feelings may be different," said Alice; "all I know is, it would feel very queer to *me*."

"You!" said the Caterpillar contemptuously. "Who are *you*?"

(Lewis Carroll, *Alice in Wonderland*.)

How would you answer that question? On what or whom depends your sense of self? Are you the same from one moment to the next? Why is it important to know who you are, anyway? Why can't you just "be"?

What for Alice begins as a comical piece of circular reasoning readily becomes a serious inquiry, a philosophical quest. The French impressionist Paul Gauguin summarized all of human experience with three agonizing questions painted on his masterpiece: "Whence come we? What are we? Whither are we going?" Similarly, a good actor uses these keys to develop his character: "Who am I? What's going on here? What is my relationship to the other characters?"

No man is an Iland, intire of it selfe; every man is a peece of the continent, a part of the maine; if a Clod bee washed away by the Sea, Europe is the less, as well as if a Promontorie were, as well as if a Mannor of thy friends or of thine own were. Any mans death diminishes me, because I am involved in Mankinde. And therefore never send to know for whom the bell tolls. It tolls for thee.

John Donne, *Devotions*

I used these words of Donne, written more than three hundred years ago, to introduce the very contemporary theme of global interdependence for a whole year of integrative and collaborative learning with gifted fifth- and sixth-grade students. I wanted my class to realize that one's identity and integrity come not in isolation—just being the best—but in appreciating the insights and abilities of others as contributors to our own development.

Knowing that we are all image bearers of God goes a long way toward understanding who we are as individuals in relationship to each other and to him. The character traits of God and of prominent figures in the history of his people, contained in the Bible, are crucial clues if we would unravel the mysteries of our souls. When we know who we are, we can think about where we are coming from and where we are going. If we have some idea of what we are looking for, we are more likely to find ourselves.

An adolescent girl confided gloomily to a friend at a party, "I spent two hours today trying to figure myself out."

"Really?" interposed a young man sitting nearby. "I spend much of my time telling myself how I am!"

Where had he found his answers, his confidence and joy? In the Bible. This is not to say he will never have serious questions and decisions—that is the function of adolescence and the secret to lifelong growth as an individual—but he knows where to turn for help in his quest.

> I'm nobody! Who are you?
> Are you nobody, too?
> Then there's a pair of us—don't tell!
> They'd banish us, you know.
>
> How dreary to be somebody!
> How public, like a frog,
> To tell your name the livelong day
> To an admiring bog!
> Emily Dickinson, *I'm Nobody*

I chose to memorize this poem in sixth grade, because it was the shortest one I could find in the huge anthology in my parents' library. I passed the recitation requirement, hoping promptly to forget the poem and the whole genre of poetry, but I couldn't get it out of my mind.

Emily Dickinson lived a very isolated life, rarely leaving the protection of her home. She may even have been pathologically withdrawn. Fortunately for the depth of her development as a person and a poet, her experience was broadened by a number of her father's distinguished visitors, some of whom were quite carried away by their own distinction. In this poem, Dickinson poked fun at pretentiousness and at the same time expressed her satisfaction and safety in the modesty and honest simplicity of her own life. She also makes me consider whether I am a nobody or a somebody, and in whose eyes? Which do I want to be? Does it make any difference who *I* am, where or what *I* do in the grand scheme of things?

Every week during my two years of formal Hebrew language instruction, the response to the roll call was *Henani* (pronounced hee-nay-nee), equivalent to the English "present" or "here," but literally translated, "Here am I." When I began to study the whole Bible for myself, I became aware that many of its great characters had responded to God's call in exactly the same way, although the Hebrew *Henani* may have been altered in translation. These men made themselves available to God, each beginning from a different place and for a different purpose, but in every case rendering a total commitment. A look at the details and directions of their lives prompts me to examine my own responses to God. "Here am I" is more than an indication of my physical location; it defines my spiritual identity in relationship to the Creator who calls.

What does it mean for God to call, anyway? And to what calling are we called? His methods and his message vary from person to person, and even with the same individual at different times in his or her life, as we shall discover. God may speak in an audible voice or an internal one, or he may reveal himself visually in dreams or a flash of light. He may speak to one person directly or through another who is called to serve as his messenger. He calls to his own, and also to those who claim no affiliation with him. He calls us to faith, to worship, to obedience, to submission, to action, or to wait. When God calls, he invites us, but he does not compel us to respond.

Why do people not respond when called by God or by another person? We can come up with all kinds of excuses, mostly centered around ourselves. We get bogged down in the particulars of our lives, "busy here and there" (1 Kings 20:40), and miss the bigger picture of his plan. With our heads in the diaper pail or mop bucket, eyes glued to the computer screen, or thoughts caught up in the tinsel of our materialistic society, readily hearkening to the clanging bells of consumerism, we become deaf to the still small voice of the almighty God (1 Kings 19:12).

It is not necessary to stop all activity to hear God's call. We don't need to go on a pilgrimage to Oz, Mecca, Tibet, or even Jerusalem to find answers to our problems. But we do need to listen. God is calling us all the time—a twenty-four-hour broadcast. If we are not aware of his words, it is only because we have tuned him out and turned to another channel. Many of Jesus' miracles were public manifestations of his deity, open for all to see. Yet only a fraction of the crowds put their faith in him. Many turned away in disbelief, and it was meant to be so. The parables were spoken to all ears, yet understood by only a few. As Jesus said:

> Though seeing, they do not see;
> though hearing, they do not hear or understand.
> In them is fulfilled the prophecy of Isaiah:
> "You will be ever hearing but never understanding;
> you will be ever seeing but never perceiving.
> For this people's heart has become calloused;
> they hardly hear with their ears,
> and they have closed their eyes.
> Otherwise they might see with their eyes,
> hear with their ears,
> understand with their hearts
> and turn, and I would heal them" (Matt. 13:13–15).

God calls continually, but too often we fail to respond. We are not hard of hearing, but hard of heart.

Still, there is hope. As we turn to study the lives of real people in the Bible, we will be challenged to examine our own lives. Though several of them are categorized as patriarchs, these Old Testament figures were not paradigms of perfection. Far from it! They were wholly human, just as we are, with the same character flaws and temptations. Their struggles with personal identity were similar to our own. And through each individual study we shall discover a different aspect of the nature of God, for he calls particular people to himself while he is fully cognizant of their unique needs and gifts. We will also find an array of different attitudes reflected in these persons' common response *"Henani"* because of their different personalities and situations.

The English sequence of the words *Here am I* is sufficiently unfamiliar to call attention to itself. It strikes me that if the order were *I am here*, the focus would be on the location of the speaker—here, as opposed to someplace else. If it read *Here I am*, the emphasis would be on present existence—alive, real, now. But with the *I* coming at the end, *I* carries the stress in the phrase, highlighting the essential being, the personality and uniqueness of the one responding.

As we shall discover, our God is very personal, both in his own nature and in his consideration of our needs and our faith. His hand sweeps across centuries, ordering entire galaxies according to his will, but he deals with his children one at a time. Because we belong to him, it is impossible for us to slip between the cracks of world history. Jesus promised, "My sheep listen to my voice; I know them, and they follow me. I give them eternal life, and they shall never perish; no one can snatch them out of my hand. My Father, who has given them to me, is greater than all; no one can snatch them out of my Father's hand" (John 10:27–29). Each precious sheep, known and called individually, is safe in his arms.

In studying the lives of these men of Scripture, we will learn how diverse a band of individuals God has gathered to himself. Without giving up their uniqueness, they found self-fulfillment as they answered God's call with the same phrase. Although the various aspects of their personalities were highlighted in their special trials and triumphs, their common answer points out the response each one of us can make to the Lord. To paraphrase St. Augustine, each one of us has a God-shaped hole within us, such that we cannot truly find ourselves until we give ourselves up to find completeness in him.

Before we can become acquainted with the men who said *Henani*, and a few who did not, we need to understand the meaning of the term and appreciate the challenge of Bible translation. To begin on a personal level, pretend your telephone is ringing right now and you are about to answer it. What will you say? Hello is the most popular answer in the United States, so I will guess you will put down this book, pick up the receiver, and say hello. Then, after the caller identifies herself as a good friend, you will probably repeat the greeting in a variant form: "Oh, hi, Joan. How are you?" But if you find that the caller is a stranger, either because you don't recognize his voice or because he mispronounces your name, and you suspect he may be trying to sell you something, you change your tone. "Yes. This is Mrs. Buswell. What can I do for you?" Or "How may I help you," or "What is it?" In France the standard form of greeting changes according to the time of day: *Good day*, or *Good evening*. In the Far East the response depends on the relative age, position, and relationship of the two parties. In Italy the common answer is *Pronto*, which means "Ready," whether or not you are ready.

Now suppose someone called your name from the next room. Depending on your guess as to who was speaking and why, you might answer, "Hmm?" "What is it?" "Here," "Pardon me?" "Yes?" "I'm in the living room," or nothing at all. You could have several reasons for each choice, which all mean approximately, but not exactly, the same thing. If someone responded to a call with the words, "At your service, sir," we would immediately draw some conclusions, which could turn out to be either right or wrong. We might suppose the speaker was a British butler from a 1930s movie, or that he was a friend playing a joke on us. The rest of the conversation would give us more clues.

In fact, this last, most formal statement of availability for service comes closest to being a literal translation of the Hebrew term *Henani;* but you won't find those words in any English version of the Bible, because they convey an artificial stiffness that is inappropriate. Instead, there should be a subtle and natural fitting of the phrase to the context of the relationship, like the distinction between "Hello," "Hi," and "How do you do?" *Henani* literally expresses the attitude of a slave who desires to do whatever the master bids. It conveys respect and honor without pompousness or groveling; a proper sense of humility and integrity, as well as loyalty and energy to serve well, are also implied.

A career as a translator is a fascinating one, because each language has its own set of assumptions. There are many idioms and inflections that lose their meaning if they are translated word for word. In good translation more than a language barrier is crossed; an entirely new cultural context is entered. It is not just a question of using a dictionary but of having a whole frame of mind, a world view.

While it is interesting to discover that phrases translated "Here I am," "Yes, my son," and so forth, in the King James or New International Versions of the Bible all express the same Hebrew words in the original manuscripts, that discovery is not the end of the lessons we can learn from this book. That observation was a useful insight in designing this series of studies, since it provided a common theme from which to begin to explore the personalities and situations of these individuals; but in and of itself the phrase carries no force for our lives. We can say, "Oh, how interesting," and drop the matter right there. What I hope will happen instead is that you will first consider these people's responses to God as keys to understanding their lives. Second, I anticipate that you will become more aware of God's character as caller, both to those men in the Old Testament and to yourself today. And third, I challenge you to examine your own attitudes as you choose whether, when, and how to respond to him.

> Just as I am, without one plea,
> But that thy blood was shed for me,
> And that thou bidd'st me come to thee,
> O Lamb of God, I come! I come!
>
> Just as I am, and waiting not
> To rid my soul of one dark blot,
> To thee whose blood can cleanse each spot,
> O Lamb of God, I come! I come!
>
> Just as I am, though tossed about
> With many a conflict, many a doubt,
> Fightings and fears within, without,
> O Lamb of God, I come! I come!
>
> Just as I am, poor, wretched, blind;
> Sight, riches, healing of the mind,
> Yea, all I need, in thee I find,
> O Lamb of God, I come! I come!
>
> Just as I am, thou wilt receive,
> Wilt welcome, pardon, cleanse, relieve;
> Because thy promise I believe,
> O Lamb of God, I come! I come!
>
> Charlotte Elliott, 1836

2

Adam
The Shame of Self

Primary Scripture Reading

Genesis 1–5

Supplementary References

Psalms 8, 14, 103, 139
Heb. 2:14–15

Questions for Study and Discussion

1. Read Genesis 1–5 carefully. Why did God create Adam? Why did he create Eve? What did he command them to do and not to do?

2. Why did God allow the "forbidden fruit" tree to be in the perfect Garden of Eden? Or the serpent, for that matter?

3. Identify the conversations in these chapters. They took place between which speakers? Exactly what questions did God ask, and of whom? Why? What answers were given? What was accomplished by the questioning?

4. What is shame? Does it serve any useful purpose, do you think? Who felt shame in Genesis 3? Who did not? Why? What solutions were put into effect? Under what circumstances have you experienced the shame of self? How was it resolved?

5. The privilege of making choices is God's special gift to humankind. What choices are you making now? Are you accepting responsibility for your choices, or are you blaming others for the consequences of your actions?

6. What questions is God asking you? What are you learning as you answer? Are you hiding? Why? When God comes after you with questions, how will you handle his love and his invitation to forgiveness and fellowship?

H ave you ever asked a question to which you already knew the answer? Of course you have, and I just did! The habit offers not only a chance to be coy or to show off, but also an invitation to the respondent to come up with her own answers. Parents and teachers do this all the time, sometimes effectively. As an alternative to straight lecturing, questioning techniques credit the listener with the ability to engage in independent thought, giving him or her a participatory rather than a passive role in the learning and growing process.

Wise parents understand the difference between meaningful and frustrating choices, depending on the age of the child and the issues involved. "Do you want to go to the zoo?" is worth asking only if the child has real input into the decision. If he is going to be dragged willy-nilly, or if there is no chance of going no matter what he desires, it is better not to bring up the subject. "Would you like to wear your sweater or your jacket?" is better than "Do you think you need a sweater?" if a negative answer to the second question will be unacceptable in the parents' view.

The Secret Seed

God did not create out of a sense of loneliness or incompleteness, but as a manifestation of his wonderful creative essence. When he created male and female after his own image, he had in mind a special relationship between himself and humankind not possible with any other creature. True fellowship always involves choice—the voluntary determination to share and be and do together. God knew the risks he took in giving us free will, permitting us to make our own choices independent of and contrary to the ideal path of perfect peace. Perhaps the most significant aspect of humanity's creation was this possibility and promise of choice, this opportunity to experience true fellowship with God himself—not mere instinct or preprogramming, not forced labor, but real love.

God's love of humanity is evident from his design of the universe, from the work and privileges he assigned, and from his suitable shaping of Adam's helpmeet. Before he formed man out of the dust, he created out of nothing an appropriate, organized environment in which we could not just survive, but thrive. He provided air and food to sustain our bodies, and abundant beauty to nourish our souls—joyfully elaborating on what could have been a meagerly adequate black-and-white, cornflakes-for-breakfast and peanut-butter-and-jelly world—all for our delight and to the praise of his glory. He planned with perfect forethought a world fit for human habitation, and a human form fit for divine participation in that world. Isn't it wonderful to ponder that God's intention from the beginning of creation was never perfection, but redemption!

Notice the listing in Genesis of the things Adam was to do and to be for God:

to be in God's image and likeness (1:27)
to rule over the fish, birds, livestock, earth, and creatures (1:28)
to be fruitful and multiply (1:28)
to fill the earth and subdue it (1:28)
to work and take care of the garden (2:15)
to obey God's command not to eat of the tree of the knowledge of good and evil (2:17)
to name the creatures (2:19–20)
to be united to his wife (2:24)

These duties were all assigned before his fall into sin, and none was rescinded afterward. Psalm 8 notes the mystery of our continued position in creation:

O LORD, our Lord, how majestic is your name in all the earth!
You have set your glory above the heavens.

> From the lips of children and infants you have ordained praise
>> because of your enemies, to silence the foe and the avenger.
> When I consider your heavens, the work of your fingers,
>> the moon and the stars, which you have set in place,
> what is man that you are mindful of him, the son of man that you
>> care for him?
> You made him a little lower than the heavenly beings
>> and crowned him with glory and honor.
> You made him ruler over the works of your hands;
>> you put everything under his feet:
> all flocks and herds, and the beasts of the field, the birds of the
>> air,
>> and the fish of the sea, all that swim the paths of the seas.
> O LORD, our Lord, how majestic is your name in all the earth!

To be a co-worker with God, steward of his creation, is a high calling indeed, intended from the beginning and secured forever, not by our own merit, but by the best promise of God himself in the person of Jesus Christ. The seed of this promise is planted in Genesis 3:15. At our darkest moment, when each of us is brought face to face with our own disobedience and defiance of God, he still offers us his light and life and love.

Eve was no afterthought made from recycled parts. Rather, God was saving the best for last, waiting for Adam to name the animals and thus to recognize his need for unique intimate relationship. Only then was she provided from his own flesh and bone, the perfect partner. This first couple was to be the rationale and the model for all marriage, and for God's expression of his permanent commitment to his people: "For this reason a man will leave his father and mother and be united to his wife, and they will become one flesh" (Gen. 2:24).

The Shame of Self

The honeymoon of joy and bliss in Eden did not last long, however, and it seems clear that it was not intended to. Have you ever wondered why God seemingly spoiled, or at least short-circuited, the perfection of Paradise by placing the tree of the knowledge of good and evil within the garden in the first place? Wouldn't it have been easier to guarantee the success of the first couple—to preclude the possibility of sin by eliminating all temptation?

On the other hand, Paradise was not booby-trapped for our inevitable doom. To have meaning, Eden had to offer humankind a choice between real alternatives: good versus evil, true versus false, life versus death. God did not sadistically set us up in order to knock us down; however, it is necessary for each of us to recognize our real position, our fallen state, before we can take the first step toward responding to God. It is not so much the issue of original sin that is important to us within the scope of this study, but the origin of shame, which must be transformed into true humility before we can fully enjoy and serve our Lord.

Why begin this study with Adam, who did *not* say to God, "Here am I"? Because each one of us still *is* Adam, stuck with the same self-shame that he experienced, that we have inherited from him, and that we repeat out of our own personal weakness. We must understand his shame, our shame, before we can appreciate and accept God's grace in drawing us to himself.

Webster's *Third New International Unabridged Dictionary* defines shame as "a painful emotion caused by consciousness of guilt, shortcoming, or impropriety in one's own behavior or position or in the behavior or position of a closely associated person or group." Each one of us has, no doubt, experienced shame at some point in our lives, and perhaps feels ashamed at this moment, although it would be impolite for me to suggest we add to that pain by bringing it up for public discussion. Two comments should be made, however. First, Genesis 2:25 states that there was a time when shame was not part of the human condition: "The man and his wife were both naked, and they felt no shame." What brought the sense of shame was their sin, specifically their eating from the tree which God had set off limits:

Then the eyes of both of them were opened, and they realized they were naked; so they sewed fig leaves together and
made coverings for themselves.

Then the man and his wife heard the sound of the LORD God as
he was walking in the garden in the cool of the day, and they hid
from the LORD God among the trees of the garden (Gen. 3:7–8).

Look carefully at the verbs in the passage, which indicate the
sequence of events in the scene:

the eyes of both of them *were opened*
they *realized* they were naked
so they *sewed* fig leaves together and *made coverings*
then the man and his wife *heard* the sound of the LORD
and they *hid* from the LORD God

We could summarize the action as follows: awareness, attempt,
avoidance. Upon eating the fruit, Adam and Eve suddenly became aware of themselves in a new way. They were now self-
conscious, exposed, ashamed before one another and before
God. With their deliberate disobedience came the sense of separation. First they sought to cover their outward nakedness, but
this was not enough. Whereas formerly they had enjoyed the
time of fellowship with God as he walked in the garden in the
cool of the day, now when they heard him coming, they hid.
Still, God found them:

But the LORD God called to the man, "Where are you?"

He answered, "I heard you in the garden, and I was afraid
because I was naked; so I hid."

And he said, "Who told you that you were naked? Have you
eaten from the tree that I commanded you not to eat from?"

The man said, "The woman you put here with me—she gave
me some fruit from the tree, and I ate it."

Then the LORD God said to the woman, "What is this you
have done?"

The woman said, "The serpent deceived me, and I ate."

So the LORD God said to the serpent, "Because you have done
this . . ." (Gen. 3:9–14).

So quickly the helpmeet became the scapegoat, as Adam blamed both Eve and God for his own disobedience. Eve in turn blamed the serpent, who wasn't given time to make any excuses before God intervened.

Consider the four direct questions put by God:

"Where are you?"
"Who told you that you were naked?"
"Have you eaten from the tree that I commanded you not to eat from?"
"What is this you have done?"

Our omniscient, omnipotent God doesn't need any part of his creation to tell him anything about our location ("Where?"), or the identity of the tempter ("Who?"), or what we have done. So why did he ask? For the same reason he asks each one of us today: to let us consider for ourselves our position in relation to him, and to remind us that we cannot and do not need to hide from him, "for he knows how we are formed, he remembers that we are dust" (Ps. 103:14). Psalm 139 puts these thoughts in the context of praise:

O LORD, you have searched me and you know me.
You know when I sit and when I rise; you perceive my thoughts from afar.
You discern my going out and my lying down; you are familiar with all my ways.
Before a word is on my tongue you know it completely, O LORD.
You hem me in—behind and before; you have laid your hand upon me.
Such knowledge is too wonderful for me, too lofty for me to attain.
Where can I go from your Spirit? Where can I flee from your presence? (Ps. 139:1–7).

The Solution

Sin, guilt, punishment, death—these all had their origins in Genesis 3. We must daily face the fact of our fallen state. Yet we

31

need not feel that all is lost forever, that there is no hope, no purpose, no way out of our misery. Jesus Christ loves us to the uttermost and has vanquished the tempter in our behalf: "Since the children have flesh and blood, he too shared in their humanity so that by his death he might destroy him who holds the power of death—that is, the devil—and free those who all their lives were held in slavery by their fear of death" (Heb. 2:14–15). He invites us to confess, not because he wants to embarrass us, but that he might forgive, that our fellowship with him might be restored, that we might find freedom from fear.

The second point to be made about shame is that it has a place and a purpose at the beginning of our walk with God. Adam and Eve needed to experience the pain of their separation from God, as a first step toward genuine fellowship. The story of the fall did not spell the end for humankind, but the setting of the stage for our development. The gates of Paradise are locked and guarded now, but a new and living way is opened for us through Jesus Christ (Heb. 10:20). Adam and Eve were not wiped off the face of the earth. There were grave consequences of their disobedience, but also perfect provision for their needs. God himself made garments of skin to cover them (Gen. 3:21), a foreshadowing of the complete covering for sin by the sacrifice of his Son. The human line, still in the image of God, was continued, not through either Cain or Abel, but through Seth, as Genesis 5 reminds us:

> This is the written account of Adam's line.
> When God created man, he made him in the likeness of God. He created them male and female and blessed them. At the time they were created, he blessed them and called them "man."
> When Adam had lived 130 years, he had a son in his own likeness, in his own image; and he named him Seth. After Seth was born, Adam lived 800 years and had other sons and daughters. Altogether, Adam lived 930 years, and then he died (Gen. 5:1–5).

When God came into the garden with questions, it was not because he needed answers. Nor was he practicing a rhetorical device or a pedantic exercise. Rather, he was acting as a loving father to help Adam find his way back. Adam did not answer *Henani*, but we can. When we try to hide, we miss out on the healing that can come only when we speak up from behind the feeble fig leaves of our own puny efforts. It is not that God by that vocal hint can suddenly find us, but that we can begin to find ourselves where we are, humbled but not humiliated by our loving Lord.

Perhaps you feel a sense of shame before God today. It is likely that you do, in fact, since "there is no one who does good" (Ps. 14:3). But do not let that feeling of disgrace and defeat keep you from the joy of continued relationship. For each of us whom God calls, it is not enough for us to respond, "I have sinned; I am ashamed and therefore I cannot answer you." We are created as human beings, not ostriches. God knows our sin just as he knew Adam's, and he calls to us today in the same way he called to the first man. He understands our sense of shame; in fact, he plants it within our consciences to guide us gently back to him.

As we go on to consider how other men did answer God's call, may we be encouraged by the awareness of God's intimate knowledge and ultimate love as he invites us to enjoy permanent fellowship with him.

> Search me, O God, and know my heart today;
> Try me, O Savior, know my thoughts, I pray.
> See if there be some wicked way in me;
> Cleanse me from every sin and set me free.
>
> I praise Thee, Lord, for cleansing me from sin;
> Fulfill thy Word and make me pure within.
> Fill me with fire where once I burned with shame;
> Grant my desire to magnify thy name.
>
> Lord, take my life and make it wholly thine;
> Fill my poor heart with thy great love divine.
> Take all my will, my passion, self, and pride;
> I now surrender, Lord—in me abide.

O Holy Spirit, revival comes from thee;
Send a revival—start the work in me.
Thy Word declares thou wilt supply our need;
For blessings now, O Lord, I humbly plead.

J. Edwin Orr, 1936

3

Abraham
The Sacrifice of Self

Primary Scripture Reading

Genesis 11–25

Supplementary References

John 3:16
Romans 4:9–13, 8:28, 9:7–9
Galatians 4
Hebrews 11

Questions for Study and Discussion

1. Why did God call Abraham out of Ur? What did he promise him? What did he ask of Abraham in return?

2. Note various occasions on which God spoke to Abraham or Abraham spoke to God. What strikes you as especially interesting about these conversations and the relationship they reflect?

3. Trace the stages in the elaboration of God's covenant and commands to Abraham.

4. Abraham used the term *Henani* three times, more than any other biblical person did. In which chapter do these utterances occur? What, do you think, did Abraham mean by this phrase? Was his meaning the same when he said it to God as when he said it to Isaac?

5. In what ways were Ishmael and Isaac similar? What distinctions did God make between them? Why? Why was Isaac referred to as Abraham's only son? Why was he the only thing God asked Abraham to sacrifice? In what ways are you a child of Abraham?

6. Who or what was really sacrificed in Genesis 22? What significance does this passage have for you? Have you ever been asked to sacrifice anything? What? By whom? How did you respond? What is God asking of you now? How are you responding to his call?

The first person recorded in the Bible to have said *Henani* in response to God's call was Abraham. But this is not to say that Abraham *always* answered God with this phrase, nor that God *only* called him to elicit this response. Abraham's biography spans fifteen chapters of Genesis, covering 175 years and many separate adventures. God spoke to him, and he spoke to God often, but not always at the outset of a project. His interactions and intrigues within his family and in his world are fairly familiar, both as positive and negative illustrations, from our Sunday-school lessons.

And through past studies of Abraham, probably most of us have also made the acquaintance of Sarah, Hagar, Lot, Isaac, Ishmael, Abimelech, a pharaoh, Eliezer, and Melchizedek. Their names may look and sound odd to us, but their stories are familiar if we know anything about the life of Abraham. God guided them as well, revealing himself to them in dreams, appearances, and circumstances, whether they appealed to him in faith or resisted him out of fear. We are told that "the angel of the LORD found Hagar" when she ran from Sarah (Gen. 16:7), and later that "God heard [Ishmael] crying and the angel of God called to Hagar from heaven" (Gen. 21:17). Two angels bodily delivered Lot and his daughters from Sodom (Gen. 19). God warned Abimelech in a dream not to harm Abraham's wife Sarah, even though the patriarch had tried to pass her off as his sister (Gen. 20). Melchizedek was apparently "priest of God Most High" long before he blessed Abraham in his name (Gen. 14:18–20). God answered Eliezer's prayer to the "LORD, the God of my master Abraham" for guidance in recognizing the wife chosen for Isaac (Gen. 24:27). But though God intervened in each of their lives, to none of these figures is ascribed the answer

Henani. Only Abraham spoke this phrase; in fact, he used it three times altogether, all within a few hours in a single chapter of his long life. If we can understand when and why Abraham said *Henani,* we will have learned something significant about the sacrifice of self.

Empty Hands

Ten times God spoke to Abraham. The first call and promise are recorded in Genesis 12:1–3.

> The LORD had said to Abram, "Leave your country, your people and your father's household and go to the land I will show you.
> "I will make you into a great nation and I will bless you;
> I will make your name great, and you will be a blessing.
> I will bless those who bless you, and whoever curses you I will curse;
> and all peoples on earth will be blessed through you."[1]

Notice that God did not ask Abram whether he was willing to leave his home and family and go to an unknown land, with or without blessings. Abram gave no verbal assent, he just went, putting his faith on the line very powerfully but simply: "So Abram left, as the LORD had told him" (Gen. 12:4). Abram's only assignment was to go; the rest of the contract consisted of God's actions—to show, to make, to bless, and to curse. When Abram arrived in Canaan, "the LORD appeared to Abram and said, 'To your offspring I will give this land'" (Gen 12:7), adding yet another verb to his own obligation. Abram's response was again only a consequence, not a condition: "So he built an altar there to the LORD, who had appeared to him."

God reiterated this gift in the next chapter:

> The LORD said to Abram after Lot had parted from him, "Lift up your eyes from where you are and look north and south, east

---

1. See Gen. 17:5, 15, where God changed the names of Abram and Sarai to Abraham and Sarah. These differences are significant, and are followed here in accordance with their spelling in the appropriate texts. When referring to the individual as a whole person, the latter spelling will be used.

and west. All the land that you see I will give to you and your offspring forever. I will make your offspring like the dust of the earth, so that if anyone could count the dust, then your offspring could be counted. Go, walk through the length and breadth of the land, for I am giving it to you" (Gen. 13:14–17).

And again, Abram responded with action: "So Abram moved his tents and went to live near the great trees of Mamre at Hebron, where he built an altar to the LORD" (Gen. 13:18).

Similarly, the further elaborations of God's covenant with Abram show it to be a unilateral agreement—what God committed himself to do for and through Abram. Abram, after all, had nothing to offer in return, except faith in the one who promised, and this was considered sufficient: "Abram believed the LORD, and he credited it to him as righteousness" (Gen. 15:6). Hebrews 11:11 describes the same occasion in these words: "By faith Abraham, even though he was past age—and Sarah herself was barren—was enabled to become a father because he considered him faithful who had made the promise." Abraham demonstrated his faith through his immediate action when the requirement of circumcision was later added to the covenant: "On that very day Abraham took his son Ishmael and all those born in his household or bought with his money, every male in his household, and circumcised them, as God told him" (Gen. 17:23). Romans 4:9–13 reiterates that it was for Abraham's faith, not for the act of circumcision, however, that righteousness was credited to him.

On the next occasion, "the LORD appeared to Abraham near the great trees of Mamre while he was sitting at the entrance to his tent in the heat of the day" (Gen. 18:1). God had a twofold purpose to this visit: to include Abraham's wife Sarah directly in the promise of a child, and to confide to Abraham God's plans regarding Sodom. The faith of this couple was encouraged to grow, but no verbal or physical stake was demanded. Abraham still had nothing to offer.

Full Hands

God spoke to Abraham for the eighth time in Genesis 21. The opening verses of that chapter note a major change in the family, with emphasis on the fulfillment of God's promise:

> Now the LORD was gracious to Sarah as he had said, and the LORD did for Sarah what he had *promised*. Sarah became pregnant and bore a son to Abraham in his old age, at the very time God had *promised* him. Abraham gave the name Isaac to the son Sarah bore him. When his son Isaac was eight days old, Abraham circumcised him, as God commanded him (Gen. 21:1–4, italics added).

Suddenly, Abraham had something of his own, a son brought from his own loins and the quickened body of his wife. The circumcision of Isaac represented Abraham's enlistment of this offspring into God's covenant by the prescribed sign, just as he and his first child Ishmael had already joined by obedience. Faith was demonstrated once again in prompt, overt action.

Even though both Isaac and Ishmael could call Abraham Father, and both were circumcised, a clear distinction was made in their status. Ishmael was the "child of the maidservant," the product of human planning, while Isaac was the miracle baby, the "child of promise." This difference was felt from the moment of Ishmael's conception by Hagar, and carried on by Sarah, who insisted on the physical separation of the two boys the instant that she saw Ishmael mocking her son. God supported her cause, and explained the consistency of his promise to Abraham:

> The matter distressed Abraham greatly because it concerned his son [Ishmael]. But God said to him, "Do not be so distressed about the boy and your maidservant. Listen to whatever Sarah tells you, because it is through Isaac that your offspring will be reckoned. I will make the son of the maidservant into a nation also, because he is your offspring" (Gen. 21:11–13).

The distinction between Ishmael and Isaac is maintained throughout the Scriptures, and becomes not only a rationale for identity among God's chosen people (Israel), but also a symbol of the inclusion of everyone in God's family by faith in his promises.

> For not all who are descended from Israel are Israel. Nor because they are his descendants are they all Abraham's children. On the contrary, "It is through Isaac that your offspring will be reckoned." In other words, it is not the natural children who are God's children, but it is the children of the promise who are regarded as Abraham's offspring. For this was how the promise was stated: "At the appointed time I will return, and Sarah will have a son" (Rom. 9:7–9).

Similarly, the whole of Galatians 4 deserves careful study to see how Paul used the two lines of Abraham's descendants to prove the believer's position as a true heir of Christ. The point we need to have clear in our minds now is that Abraham produced Ishmael by his own efforts, but Ishmael was not the "true son." Isaac's conception was made possible only by a multiple miracle of God, yet he *was* the "promised seed" (singular), and Abraham's "one and only son," his *own*. Finally, Abraham had something to give up to God.

Empty Hands Again

Now we are ready to examine Genesis 22 in depth.

> Some time later God tested Abraham. He said to him, "Abraham!"
> "Here I am [*Henani*]," he replied.
> Then God said, "Take your son, your only son, Isaac, whom you love, and go to the region of Moriah. Sacrifice him there as a burnt offering on one of the mountains I will tell you about" (Gen. 22:1–2).

We won't belabor the point that God did not *tempt* Abraham here, but only tested him, and that not for purposes of God's own research, but for Abraham's sake—to develop his faith and confidence in the character of God. Here at last is the occasion of Abraham's first use of that response *Henani*, which we have set out to trace. While leaving room for the possibility that he might have used it in other instances that were not recorded in the Bible, it is significant that Abraham's whole history may be summarized as a search for self in his seed, which has finally been straightened out in the preceding chapter of Genesis.

God's original call had included the promise of a "great nation" to come. The future was still very much on Abraham's mind when God appeared in a vision, saying, "Do not be afraid, Abram. I am your shield, your very great reward," so that all Abram could think of in response was, "'O Sovereign LORD, what can you give me since I remain childless and the one who will inherit my estate is Eliezer of Damascus?' And Abram said, 'You have given me no children; so a servant in my household will be my heir'" (Gen. 15:1–3). The plot to produce Ishmael was the result of human self-reliance, a detour from the road to faith.

Isaac was the true fulfillment of God's promise, for when God commanded Abraham to sacrifice Isaac, he emphasized four times that he was "your son, your only son, Isaac, whom you love," to make sure Abraham understood the seriousness of the command.

As usual, Abraham responded with prompt action.

Early the next morning Abraham got up and saddled his donkey. He took with him two of his servants and his son Isaac. When he had cut enough wood for the burnt offering, he set out for the place God had told him about. On the third day Abraham looked up and saw the place in the distance. He said to his servants, "Stay here with the donkey while I and the boy go over there. We will worship and then we will come back to you."

Abraham took the wood for the burnt offering and placed it on his son Isaac, and he himself carried the fire and the knife. As the two of them went on together, Isaac spoke up and said to his father Abraham, "Father?"

"Yes, my son [*Henani*]?" Abraham replied.

"The fire and wood are here," Isaac said, "but where is the lamb for the burnt offering?"

Abraham answered, "God himself will provide the lamb for the burnt offering, my son." And the two of them went on together (Gen. 22:3–8).

The straightforwardness of the text precludes a melodramatic interpretation of this scene. Abraham did not turn pale or perspire as he and Isaac approached "the place." Nor did he stall or "beat around the bush" hoping desperately for a way out. There is only confidence in his simple statement to the servants that he and his son would worship and return, and only confidence in his reply to Isaac that God would himself provide the lamb for sacrifice, as he had said.

Abraham must have considered the possibility that God would actually require Isaac to serve as the lamb in the fullest sense of living sacrifice, since that had been the command. After all, do not we humans generally function on this assumption of consistency, rather than contradiction, in natural and spiritual events? Even in the dialogue about Sodom in Genesis 18, the net result was not the changing of God's mind, but the revealing of the quality of his justice and mercy to Abraham and to us. Abraham knew what God had said; he also knew that God keeps his word. If God in his infinite wisdom wanted Isaac to become Abraham's heir by dying first, then so be it. Abraham believed God's promises and his power to accomplish his purposes, and for the most part Abraham accepted and lived according to them, even though he could not always comprehend them.

> By faith Abraham, when God tested him, offered Isaac as a sacrifice. He who had received the promises was about to sacrifice his one and only son, even though God had said to him, "It is through Isaac that your offspring will be reckoned." Abraham reasoned that God could raise the dead, and figuratively speaking he did receive Isaac back from death" (Heb. 11:17–19).

This does not mean that the test was any the less real or painful for Abraham, nor that "knowing everything would work out somehow" (as we sometimes foolishly paraphrase Rom. 8:28) made it any easier for him to tie up his son and reach for the knife, as the next verses describe:

When they reached the place God had told him about, Abraham built an altar there and arranged the wood on it. He bound his son Isaac and laid him on the altar, on top of the wood. Then he reached out his hand and took the knife to slay his son. But the angel of the LORD called out to him from heaven, "Abraham! Abraham!"

"Here I am [*Henani*]," he replied.

"Do not lay a hand on the boy," he said. "Do not do anything to him. Now I know that you fear God, because you have not withheld from me your son, your only son."

Abraham looked up and there in a thicket he saw a ram caught by its horns. He went over and took the ram and sacrificed it as a burnt offering instead of his son. So Abraham called that place "the LORD will provide." And to this day it is said, "On the mountain of the LORD it will be provided."

The angel of the LORD called to Abraham from heaven a second time and said, "I swear by myself, declares the LORD, that because you have done this and have not withheld your son, your only son, I will surely bless you and make your descendants as numerous as the stars in the sky and as the sand on the seashore. Your descendants will take possession of the cities of their enemies, and through your offspring all nations on earth will be blessed, because you have obeyed me."

Then Abraham returned to his servants and they set off together for Beersheba. And Abraham stayed in Beersheba (Gen. 22:9–19).

When Abraham responded to Isaac's question by saying *Henani*, he was affirming that his own life was bound up in his son, that *here*, in fact, *was he*. Although we sometimes take a shortcut by referring to this chapter as "The Sacrifice of Isaac," clearly Isaac was never sacrificed. It was really Abraham who put his *own* life on the line, and received it back again from God.

Our purpose in establishing that Isaac was Abraham's own son, rather than Ishmael, was not merely to prove that Abraham could return that possession to God, from whom he had come. God knows our hands are empty, too, and each of us must recognize the fact that we have nothing of substance to offer him, only faith in the full atoning sacrifice of his own beloved Son (John 3:16).

The point is that we are not merely to take the half-step of the hymn phrase, "We give thee but thine own," but rather to take the step of total sacrifice: "I give thee *all* of me, my *entire* self." This was the core of God's test of Abraham. He puts the same question to each one of us today. What will you put on the line for him, and what are you holding back?

> When I survey the wondrous cross,
> On which the prince of glory died,
> My richest gain I count but loss,
> And pour contempt on all my pride.
>
> Forbid it, Lord, that I should boast,
> Save in the death of Christ, my God;
> All the vain things that charm me most,
> I sacrifice them to His blood.
>
> See, from his head, his hands, His feet,
> Sorrow and love flow mingled down;
> Did e'er such love and sorrow meet,
> Or thorns compose so rich a crown?
>
> Were the whole realm of nature mine,
> That were a present far too small;
> Love so amazing, so divine,
> Demands my soul, my life, my all.
>
> Isaac Watts, 1707

4

Isaac
The Suspicious Self

Primary Scripture Reading

Genesis 17–18, 21–28

Supplementary Reference

Romans 8:28

Questions for Study and Discussion

1. Scan the above Scripture chapters to identify the most significant events in Isaac's life. List each event, and choose an adjective to describe Isaac's character as revealed in each one.

Reference	Event	Character Trait

2. Consider Isaac in his roles as brother, son, husband, neighbor, and father. How did each person react to him? How did he react to each one? Whom did he trust?

3. Read Genesis 27 closely. Write down each character's action and motivation through this chapter.

Character	Action	Motivation

4. Who said *Henani* in this chapter? Consider various attitudes reflected by this phrase as used by each character.

5. At what point(s) in his life did Isaac respond to God's call? What change(s) took place? How do you recognize God's call to you through circumstances?

6. What warning(s) from Isaac's life can you apply to your own response to God? What helps you overcome old patterns of personality and behavior? When have you rejoiced, knowing God is at work in your life?

Proper names in the Bible usually denote important character traits or events in persons' lives, and name changes are always significant. The subject of this chapter lived between two men who experienced the most life-changing name changes in all of the Old Testament—his father Abram/Abraham, and his son Jacob/Israel. Isaac's own name, which means "he laughs," was chosen by God (Gen. 17:19) to commemorate the responses of both Abraham (Gen. 17:17) and Sarah (Gen. 18:12–15) to the pronouncement of his miraculous coming.

But Isaac's name does not exactly fit either the personality or the history of its bearer who, as we shall discover, was unusually somber, self-centered, suspicious, and only submissive at the end to the will of God.

Somber

Isaac was the most passive of the patriarchs. Rather than planning and following his own course, he responded to the actions of others, sometimes wisely and sometimes not so wisely. Possibly his earliest memory was of the feast given by his parents on the occasion of his weaning, at which time his big half-brother Ishmael was seen mocking him (Gen. 21:9–10). This action precipitated the sending away of Ishmael and his mother, Hagar. The Bible suggests by its silence that the two boys did not see each other again until more than seventy years later, when they met to bury their father Abraham (Gen. 25:9). God kept his promise to care for the rejected firstborn, but his prophecy was also fulfilled: the descendants of Ishmael have continued to "live in hostility toward all his brothers" (Gen. 16:12; again in 25:18). Meanwhile, what a lasting impression must have been made on the young Isaac at his party, noticing the severe consequences of misplaced humor!

The next recorded traumatic event for Isaac was his trek up the mountainside to worship God with his father. Suddenly, Isaac asked, "The fire and wood are here, but where is the lamb for the burnt offering?" (Gen. 22:8). This episode was considered from Abraham's point of view in our preceding study. Abraham promised that "God would himself provide the lamb," and so he did, but not before Isaac was tied and laid on top of the wood and Abraham took up the knife to slay his son (Gen. 22:10). Isaac did not resist either first being tied up or then being released after God stayed his father's hand and showed him the ram in the thicket. Still, it was a most serious moment, one which Isaac undoubtedly pondered the rest of his life. It is interesting that the Bible relates no action or even a single word of Isaac's in approximately his next twenty-five years, and no further conversations between him and his father.

Meanwhile, his mother Sarah died at age 127, and Isaac's marriage to Rebekah three years later was described as a comfort for this loss (Gen. 24:67). The beautiful story of the selection of Isaac's bride by Abraham's servant stands in marked contrast to the dynamic journey of Jacob many years later to choose his own wife Rachel. Isaac did not seem to have the energy or inclination to go on his own marriage mission. His approach to life was more reflective, more passive.

Even conflicts with his enemies were initiated by aliens, not by Isaac himself, whether he was right or wrong in his position. It was Abimelech who confronted him in the matter of passing off Rebekah as his sister (Gen. 26), a repetition of an old trick Abraham had used twice without success (Gen. 12:10–20; 20:1–8). The envy of his enemies because of his prosperity resulted in their filling in his wells, an offense to which Isaac responded simply by moving away and reopening other wells three different times. Isaac was inclined to "go with the flow" rather than to make waves. When there was finally an end to the quarreling (Gen. 26:17–22), it was the enemies, not Isaac, who came to him and proposed a treaty that established peace (Gen. 26:26–32).

In family matters, too, Isaac played a serious but passive role. He did nothing to intervene in the sale of Esau's birthright to Jacob for a meal, and it is possible to believe he was not even aware of that transaction until much later. Again, he took no action to prevent Esau's marriage to two Hittite women, though "they were a source of grief to Isaac and Rebekah" (Gen. 26:35). Later, it was pressure from Rebekah that drove Isaac to send Jacob away to find wives "from among the daughters of Laban," his cousins.

External events shaped Isaac's life; in return, he made little impression on events or on the lives of others. Some things happened to him, but he didn't do much about them. His existence could be summarized aptly by a series of verbs in the passive voice: he was promised by God, mocked by Ishmael "sacrificed" by Abraham; his bride was chosen by Elimelech, and he was comforted by Rebekah after his mother's death; he was confronted by his enemies; and he was deceived by Rebekah and Jacob.

The most significant action taken by Isaac himself was his trembling as he blessed his sons. In that scene, recorded in Genesis 27, *Henani* was used in quick succession by all three of the characters—Esau, Isaac, and Jacob. As we explore what each man may have meant by this word, we can better evaluate the quality of our own response to God.

Self-centered and Suspicious

Before examining that passage in depth, it is important to understand the dynamic interplay of personalities and relationships established in Isaac's family from the beginning. Although Genesis 25:21 records that "Isaac prayed to the LORD on behalf of his wife, because she was barren," it was Rebekah who "went to inquire of the LORD" directly when she felt her babies jostling within her. "The LORD said to her, 'Two nations are in your womb, and two peoples from within you will be separated; one people will be stronger than the other and the older will serve the younger'" (Gen. 25:23). It is possible that Isaac did not hear about this pronouncement at the time.

Similarly, although the episode of Jacob's usurping Esau's birthright is placed in its chronological sequence in that chapter, it appears that Isaac was likewise unacquainted with the circumstances and underlying causes of this reversal in the usual priority for blessing. From what we have seen of his character earlier in his life, Isaac was not a man likely to defy God's clear commands when he knew them. Operating without such explicit instructions, however, Isaac was readily led by his own appetites.

In fact, Isaac was frequently guided by his own convenience and pleasure. He preferred Esau from the beginning, as Genesis 25:27–28 plainly states: "The boys grew up, and Esau became a skillful hunter, a man of the open country, while Jacob was a quiet man, staying among the tents. Isaac, who had a taste for wild game, loved Esau, but Rebekah loved Jacob." That taste for wild game was still uppermost in his mind when the time came for blessing:

> When Isaac was old and his eyes were so weak that he could no longer see, he called for Esau his older son and said to him, "My son."
>
> "Here I am [*Henani*]," he answered.
>
> Isaac said, "I am now an old man and don't know the day of my death. Now then, get your weapons—your quiver and bow—and go out to the open country to hunt some wild game for me. Prepare me the kind of tasty food I like and bring it to me to eat, so that I may give you my blessing before I die" (Gen. 27:1–4).

Esau dutifully presented himself to his father as one responding to a page. Isaac proposed a generous trade—a tasty meal for the blessing—and Esau happily accepted the offer, just as he had willingly traded his birthright for Jacob's tasty meal many years before. A birthright for a meal, a meal for a blessing—it was too good a deal for Esau to pass up. Perhaps he could have his cake and eat it, too! He had proven earlier that the blessing was not of primary interest to him, but if it were dropped back into his lap, why should he refuse it or even volunteer the information that he had forfeited his right to it? Silently, Esau went out to find food for his father, and a more secure future for himself.

Meanwhile, Rebekah had overheard Isaac's promise to Esau and moved quickly to maneuver her favorite son, Jacob, into position to receive that blessing. Whether it was out of her personal ambition, her determination to back the winner, or her strong faith in God's prenatal promise to her about the twins, Rebekah overruled all of Jacob's objections about the likelihood and consequences of being caught. She prepared her finest cooked-lamb dish and fresh bread for him to serve his father, covered his arms with goatskins, and dressed him in Esau's best clothing to deceive each of Isaac's functioning senses—touch, taste, and smell.

Then she handed to her son Jacob the tasty food and the bread she had made.

He went to his father and said, "My father."

"Yes, my son [*Henani*]," he answered. "Who is it?"

Jacob said to his father, "I am Esau your firstborn. I have done as you told me. Please sit up and eat some of my game so that you may give me your blessing."

Isaac asked his son, "How did you find it so quickly, my son?"

"The LORD your God gave me success," he replied.

Then Isaac said to Jacob, "Come near so I can touch you, my son, to know whether you really are my son Esau or not."

Jacob went close to his father Isaac, who touched him and said, "The voice is the voice of Jacob, but the hands are the hands of Esau." He did not recognize him, for his hands were hairy like those of his brother Esau; so he blessed him. "Are you really my son Esau?" he asked.

"I am [*Henani*]," he replied.

Then he said, "My son, bring me some of your game to eat, so that I may give you my blessing."

Jacob brought it to him and he ate; and he brought some wine and he drank. Then his father Isaac said to him, "Come here, my son, and kiss me."

So he went to him and kissed him. When Isaac caught the smell of his clothes, he blessed him and said, . . . (Gen. 27:18–27a).

Isaac's suspicious nature is evident in his cross-examination of Jacob, reminding me of Little Red Riding Hood's questions to the Big, Bad Wolf. Jacob's "I am" is his third lie and the third instance of its utterance in this chapter, once again to a selfish end. His lie was convincing, fulfilling the literal meaning of his name, "Supplanter." Isaac was persuaded, only hesitating for a moment at the discrepancy in the sound of Jacob's voice compared to that of Esau. (Rebekah had failed to coach her favorite in mimicry, though she had done everything else possible for him!) Isaac, undoubtedly drooling for his dinner by this time, reached for the platter with one hand while he blessed Jacob with the other, believing him to be his favorite firstborn:

51

"Ah, the smell of my son is like the smell of a field that the LORD
   has blessed.
May God give you of heaven's dew and of earth's richness—an
   abundance of grain and new wine.
May nations serve you and peoples bow down to you.
Be lord over your brothers, and may the sons of your mother
   bow down to you.
May those who curse you be cursed and those who bless you be
   blessed" (Gen. 27:7b–29).

Submissive

Finally, there is one good thing to be said for Isaac, and it is
his redeeming virtue. Though it was manipulated through a
sequence of self-seeking schemes by Isaac, Esau, Rebekah, and
Jacob, the bestowing of the patriarchal blessing was still a remarkable demonstration of God's sovereignty, and Isaac recognized it as such: "Isaac trembled violently and said,'Who was it,
then, that hunted game and brought it to me? I ate it just before
you came and I blessed him—and indeed he will be blessed!'"
(Gen. 27:33). That violent trembling and that exclamation are the
most powerful acts of faith in Isaac's life, fully qualifying him as a
link in the lineage of God's chosen family: "By faith Isaac blessed
Jacob and Esau in regard to their future" (Heb. 11:20). Isaac
trembled, not in rage at being deceived, but in the realization
that God had accomplished his purpose after all. Isaac's real
error was not that he gave the blessing to the wrong son, but that
he gave it to the right son for the wrong reasons. As such, it
would stick; it could not and would not be revoked, for all of
Esau's pathetic wailings, his sworn vengeance, and his feeble
attempt to get back in his parents' good graces by marrying one
of the daughters of his uncle Ishmael (Gen. 28:8–9).

The last words of Isaac recorded in the Bible reveal a man of
character and conviction, greatly changed by his experience. In
true submission to God, he re-called Jacob to his side and reiterated his blessing of this son, this time purposefully:

So Isaac called for Jacob and blessed him and commanded
him: "Do not marry a Canaanite woman. Go at once to Paddan

Aram, to the house of your mother's father Bethuel. Take a wife for yourself there, from among the daughters of Laban, your mother's brother. May God Almighty bless you and make you fruitful and increase your numbers until you become a community of peoples. May he give you and your descendants the blessing of Abraham, so that you may take possession of the land where you now live as an alien, the land God gave to Abraham." Then Isaac sent Jacob on his way. . . ." (Gen. 28:1–5).

Thus, Isaac sent Jacob to safety with strength, with specific directions, and with the sureness of faith befitting a true patriarch. His use of the phrase *God Almighty* (the Hebrew *El-Shaddai*) matched God's reference to himself when he appeared to Abram to announce the miracle birth of Isaac:

"I am God Almighty; walk before me and be blameless. I will confirm my covenant between me and you and will greatly increase your numbers . . . I will make you very fruitful. . . . I will establish my covenant as an everlasting covenant between me and you and your descendants after you for the generations to come, to be your God and the God of your descendants after you. The whole land of Canaan, where you are now an alien, I will give as an everlasting possession to you and your descendants after you; and I will be their God" (Gen. 17:1–8).

What warnings can we gain from Isaac's life? What claims and promises do we make, pretending to align ourselves with God's purposes, but in reality doing so with selfish motives? It is not enough to mouth the words *Here am I* even in response to God, when in truth we are only self-serving.

Secondly, have you been mistreated? Have people taken advantage of you, threatened or abused you, destroyed your self-confidence? Do you bear the scars of childhood trauma as open wounds that prevent you from forming healthy, whole relationships with members of your family and community? Trust in God. Tremble in acknowledgment of his perfect power and love to accomplish all of his good purposes—to overcome every obstacle—and lay down your doubts and fears at the foot of the cross, the symbol of his ultimate victory.

When Isaac finally submitted to the will of God, it was not merely out of reluctant recognition of God's superior strength. Isaac's spirit was not broken by his experience, but rather his character was established as he glorified God with his final statement. He broke out of his habitual seriousness and passivity, and overcame his suspicious nature with exuberant praise. Perhaps it was for this reason that God allowed him, but not Rebekah, to live to see Jacob return prosperous and reconciled with his brother after an absence of more than twenty years:

> Jacob came home to his father Isaac in Mamre, near Kiriath Arba (that is, Hebron), where Abraham and Isaac had stayed. Isaac lived a hundred and eighty years. Then he breathed his last and died and was gathered to his people, old and full of years. And his sons Esau and Jacob buried him (Gen. 35:27–29).

Surely it is not out of place to imagine that Isaac laughed at last!

> Hidden in the hollow of his blessed hand,
> Never foe can follow, never traitor stand;
> Not a surge of worry, not a shade of care,
> Not a blast of hurry touch the spirit there.
>
> Every joy or trial falleth from above,
> Traced upon our dial by the Sun of Love.
> We may trust him fully all for us to do;
> They who trust him wholly find him wholly true.
>
> REFRAIN:
> Stayed upon Jehovah, hearts are fully blest;
> Finding, as he promised, perfect peace and rest.
> Frances R. Havergal, 1874

5

Jacob
The Security of Self

Primary Scripture Reading

Genesis 25–37, 42–50

Supplementary Reference

Hebrews 11:21

Questions for Study and Discussion

1. Scan Jacob's biography. Make a list of the instances in which Jacob deceived or tried to take advantage of someone. When and how was he deceived? Did he have gain or loss through this behavior, do you think?

2. What were Jacob's best qualities as a man? What were his greatest achievements? Comment on the contrasts between his strengths and his weaknesses. Do you admire Jacob? Why, or why not?

3. Try to find the four major migrations of Jacob's life. In each case, was he motivated to move primarily by positive or negative factors? Why might he not have wanted to move? What concerned him about going to Egypt? Why did he insist on being brought back to Canaan for burial? How do *you* reach decisions about where to move?

4. Read the double account of God changing Jacob's name in Genesis 32 and 35. What do the two names mean? How did the name change affect Jacob (was he any different after this event)?

5. Find the three instances when Jacob said *Henani*. Do you find any progression or growth in the quality of his response? How did God mold Jacob's character throughout his life? What lessons is he teaching you in your present circumstances?

6. Bargains and blessings played an important role in Jacob's life. What do you find interesting about the namings and blessings of his children, whose descendants became the twelve tribes of Israel? Why, do you think, did the whole nation carry his new name?

Isn't he rightly named Jacob? He has deceived me these two times: He took my birthright, and now he's taken my blessing!" So cried Esau when he realized that his brother had tricked him out of his future. If ever a man fulfilled the meaning of his name in a negative way, it was Jacob. Over and over again, he became entangled in deceit. He acquired the birthright and blessing, wives and wealth, by clever conniving. On more than one occasion, he was on the receiving end of unfair deals. Bargaining was a way of life with him; Jacob used all his wits and resources to pursue his objectives bullheadedly, without regard for consequences. He seemed willing to stoop to any and all methods to get what he wanted, and he succeeded.

Surely, here was a person who needed to be taken down a notch, to be put in his proper place and perspective alongside God the almighty. So why was Jacob allowed to win a wrestling match with God? And how did he come to rest in his dependence on God, so that Hebrews 11:21 records "By faith Jacob, when he was dying, blessed each of Joseph's sons, and worshiped as he leaned on the top of his staff"?

In this chapter we will trace the sequence of Jacob's scheming. We will also follow the path of his blessings, which are even more numerous. Jacob did not learn that crime does not pay; everything he did prospered, whether he gained by good or ill means. What he did learn was that success is not enough. As we consider the three occasions when he said *Henani* at widely separated times in his life, we will better appreciate God's patient development of this wonderfully strong personality. Perhaps then we will find a clue that will help us to transform our tendency to rely on our own strength into the kind of peace and security that Jacob knew at the end of his life.

Scheming

The twins were already at loggerheads in Rebekah's womb. It was their jostling within her that drove her to inquire of the Lord. He responded, "Two nations are in your womb, and two peoples from within you will be separated; one people will be stronger than the other, and the older will serve the younger" (Gen. 25:23). Even so, the births were nearly simultaneous, with Jacob hanging onto Esau's heel (his name literally means "heelgrabber," which becomes "supplanter" or "deceiver" in a figurative sense).

That the prophecy would be fulfilled was without doubt, but the preference for one or the other son by their parents raises some very interesting questions. Was it natural, almost accidental, or was it deliberate for Rachel to favor Jacob, the homebody? Did she act in the hope of gaining something for herself by backing the winner, or out of faith in God's promise, or from a sense that she had to play a vital role in a scene that otherwise could turn out "wrong"? Was Isaac acting out of innocent ignorance, weakness, selfishness, or obstinacy in the face of God's words? Had Esau simply forgotten the earlier transaction when he had given up the birthright, which had been of no importance to him, or was he trying to "have his stew and blessing, too"? Were Jacob's protests against Rebekah's pushiness motivated by honesty and patient trust (as we shall see David waited for God to give him the kingdom), or by a desire to avoid carrying the responsibility or getting into trouble? However we answer these questions, it is clear that Jacob wasn't the first or the only member of his family to resort to subterfuge.

Jacob's first *Henani* was a lie. Not that he wasn't where he said he was, but he wasn't *who* he said he was. In fact, although Rebekah and her favorite son had carefully plotted to deceive Isaac's senses of smell, touch, and taste, it was Jacob's voice in response to his father's question, "Are you really my son Esau?" (Gen. 27:24) that nearly gave him away. With all the trouble they had gone to, one wonders whether it would have been less risky and more likely of success simply to enlighten Isaac as to God's promise and the working out of the brothers' agreement. In any case, Isaac allowed his suspicions to be assuaged and he gave Jacob the paternal blessing, still thinking he was talking to Esau:

> May God give you of heaven's dew and of earth's richness—
> an abundance of grain and new wine.
> May nations serve you and peoples bow down to you.
> Be lord over your brothers, and may the sons of your mother
> bow down to you.
> May those who curse you be cursed and those who bless you be
> blessed (Gen. 27:27–29).

As we have seen, Esau was furious to be so outflanked by his mother and brother, and he swore vengeance. I have always been fascinated that Rebekah was able to overhear his inward oath. It was her urging that got Jacob on his way to safety with her relatives in Paddan Aram, this time with real conviction behind Isaac's words of blessing (Gen. 28:1–4). Meanwhile, Esau took a third wife, in the hope of pleasing his parents (Gen. 28:8), and settled down to nurse his anger.

Even the schemer Jacob was no match for his uncle Laban, who offered free hospitality for a month and then prompted Jacob to name a wage. While it may sound generous of Laban at first glance, clearly he took full advantage of Jacob's boundless energy and love to acquire an outstanding bondsman and amass considerable wealth for himself. He was also cagey enough to unload on Jacob his elder daughter, Leah, who was no beauty and might otherwise not have been able to find a husband. Of course, God blessed Leah abundantly in the birth of six children, including Judah, the ancestor of Christ, but she always carried within her the hurt caused by her father's trickery and her husband's lack of favor. Meanwhile, Laban's ruse bound Jacob to him for an additional seven years (Gen. 29).

Successful

When he finally announced to his wives that it was time to leave Laban, Jacob summarized his servitude:

Jacob heard that Laban's sons were saying, "Jacob has taken everything our father owned and has gained all this wealth from what belonged to our father." And Jacob noticed that Laban's attitude toward him was not what it had been.

Then the LORD said to Jacob, "Go back to the land of your fathers and to your relatives, and I will be with you."

So Jacob sent word to Rachel and Leah to come out to the fields where his flocks were. He said to them, "I see that your father's attitude toward me is not what it was before, but the God of my father has been with me. You know that I've worked for your father with all my strength, yet your father has cheated me by changing my wages ten times. However, God has not allowed him to harm me. If he said, 'The speckled ones will be your wages,' then all the flocks gave birth to speckled young; and if he said, 'The streaked ones will be your wages,' then all the flocks bore streaked young. So God has taken away your father's livestock and given them to me.

"In breeding season I once had a dream in which I looked up and saw that the male goats mating with the flock were streaked, speckled or spotted. The angel of God said to me in the dream, 'Jacob.' I answered, 'Here I am [*Henani*].'" And he said, 'Look up and see that all the male goats mating with the flock are streaked, speckled or spotted, for I have seen all that Laban has been doing to you. I am the God of Bethel, where you anointed a pillar and where you made a vow to me. Now leave this land at once and go back to your native land.'"

Then Rachel and Leah replied, "Do we still have any share in the inheritance of our father's estate? Does he not regard us as foreigners? Not only has he sold us, but he has used up what was paid for us. Surely all the wealth that God took away from our father belongs to us and our children. So do whatever God has told you."

Then Jacob put his children and his wives on camels, and he drove all his livestock ahead of him, along with all the goods he had accumulated in Paddan Aram, to go to his father Isaac in the land of Canaan (Gen. 31:1–18).

The long passage above is worth quoting in full because there are several interesting points to be made from it. First, Jacob's strategy to increase his own flocks came under suspicion by his brothers-in-law. No matter how Laban changed the terms of his contract, Jacob always benefitted, and the question of who was outwitting whom lay at the bottom of Laban's "countenance" not being "toward him as before" (Gen. 31:2 KJV). The details are rather difficult to fathom, even through our present-day understanding of genetic engineering, but the principle is clear: Jacob prospered, not because of his counterscheming, but because God blessed him, and he knew it. When Laban caught up with him as he was running away, Jacob repeated his litany:

> I have been with you for twenty years now. Your sheep and goats have not miscarried, nor have I eaten rams from your flocks. I did not bring you animals torn by wild beasts; I bore the loss myself. And you demanded payment from me for whatever was stolen by day or night. This was my situation: The heat consumed me in the daytime and the cold at night, and sleep fled from my eyes. It was like this for the twenty years I was in your household. I worked for you fourteen years for your two daughters and six years for your flocks, and you changed my wages ten times. If the God of my father, the God of Abraham and the Fear of Isaac, had not been with me, you would surely have sent me away empty-handed. But God has seen my hardship and the toil of my hands, and last night he rebuked you (Gen. 31:38–42).

A second observation is that the sisters/wives' encouragement of Jacob to follow God's direction was the only recorded instance in which the two women expressed agreement about anything. Conflict between them was part of the daily harvest that ensued from Jacob's and Laban's original deceitfulness, and was carried forward into the next generation in the form of favoritism and bitter rivalry among Jacob's sons, as we shall see. Even though Jacob's spirit began to change, the consequences of his actions remained.

Third, all of Jacob's successes did not bring him either confidence or peace. Clearly, relationships in Paddan Aram were deteriorating, and it was time to move on. He sensed increasing opposition from his brothers-in-law, and probably felt that physical or material reprisals were not out of the question, given the nature and upbringing of Laban's family. But leaving meant going somewhere else, and that meant facing Esau, who at last report (twenty years before, with no news in between) was still intent on killing him. Apparently, no overtures had been made from either side toward a reconciliation. Jacob could only assume that Esau's fury was no more diminished than his own fear.

As he parted from Laban, the angels of God met him, ostensibly to offer encouragement. But although he named the place Mahanaim, which means "two camps" (Gen. 32:1–2), Jacob took little comfort from them. We see him acting "in great fear and distress" (Gen. 32:7) to divide his company and organize his caravan in such a way as both to impress Esau and to appease him. He sent gifts ahead with servants who were strictly enjoined as to what and how to speak to Esau when they met him. The next day he divided his wives and children, protectively placing Rachel and Joseph in the rear of the caravan in the hope that their lives, if any, might be spared.

During his early years at home and the twenty years with his uncle, Jacob had relied on his own talents to accomplish his goals. His relationship with God was still conditional: He acknowledged God's help in reference to his grandfather and father—"the God of my father, the God of Abraham and the Fear of Isaac" (Gen. 31:42); "the LORD your God" (Gen. 27:20); "O God of my father Abraham, God of my father Isaac, O LORD, who said to me . . ." (Gen. 32:9). Even when God appeared to him directly, to offer comfort or guidance, Jacob had difficulty incorporating those experiences into his approach to the obstacles that confronted him each day. He knew that God existed, because he had seen and spoken with him, but he trusted his own devices to solve his problems. Six times in the first vision at Bethel on his way to Paddan Aram, God identified himself as the one who would act on Jacob's behalf:

> *I* am the LORD, the God of your father Abraham and the God of
> Isaac. *I* will give you and your descendants the land on which
> you are lying. Your descendants will be like the dust of the earth,
> and you will spread out to the west and to the east, to the north
> and to the south. All peoples on earth will be blessed through
> you and your offspring. *I* am with you and will watch over you
> wherever you go, and *I* will bring you back to this land. *I* will not
> leave you until *I* have done what *I* have promised you (Gen.
> 28:13–15, italics added).

Even so, Jacob seemed to hedge on his own commitment:

> Then Jacob made a vow, saying, "If God will be with me and
> will watch over me on this journey I am taking and will give me
> food to eat and clothes to wear so that I return safely to my
> father's house, then the LORD will be my God and the stone that I
> have set up as a pillar will be God's house, and of all that you
> give me I will give you a tenth" (Gen. 28:20–22).

Twenty years later, after basking in God's blessing even while
suffering severe hardships under Laban's oppressive rule, Jacob
kept himself and his work in the center of the picture, as if by his
own efforts and endurance he had somehow earned God's recognition: "God has seen my hardship and the toil of my hands"
(Gen. 31:42). Surely you know someone, if indeed you do not
recognize yourself as one, who demonstrates this attitude: Faith
is held at a distance, its power not tapped, its miracles weakened
by the assertion that one is not merely a naked recipient of God's
blessings but somehow a participant in them.

Strong

So far we have skimmed the highlights of Jacob's life to note
his scheming nature and the successes it gained, neither of
which give him security. In so doing, we have missed a turning
point, one which Jacob himself seemed to miss, but which became the pivotal moment of his life. It occurred after he had sent
gifts ahead to intercept Esau and was waiting by the Jabbok
River.

That night Jacob got up and took his two wives, his two maidservants and his eleven sons and crossed the ford of the Jabbok. After he had sent them across the stream, he sent over all his possessions. So Jacob was left alone, and a man wrestled with him till daybreak. When the man saw that he could not overpower him, he touched the socket of Jacob's hip so that his hip was wrenched as he wrestled with the man. Then the man said, "Let me go, for it is daybreak."

But Jacob replied, "I will not let you go unless you bless me."

The man asked him, "What is your name?"

"Jacob," he answered.

Then the man said, "Your name will no longer be Jacob, but Israel, because you have struggled with God and with men and have overcome."

Jacob said, "Please tell me your name."

But he replied, "Why do you ask my name?" Then he blessed him there.

So Jacob called the place Peniel, saying, "It is because I saw God face to face, and yet my life was spared."

The sun rose above him as he passed Peniel, and he was limping because of his hip. Therefore to this day the Israelites do not eat the tendon attached to the socket of the hip, because the socket of Jacob's hip was touched near the tendon (Gen. 32:22–32).

Without meaning to be irreverent, this scene reminds me of the Irish legend about catching a leprechaun to get three wishes. The essential message seems to be "Besting brings blessing." But there are some interesting twists to the tale. After a night-long clinch, Jacob was apparently winning, or at least he was not losing. The man, or the angel, did not give in to Jacob's human strength, however, but dislocated his hip by the touch of a hand. That touch would certainly have turned the fight in favor of the angel, but it was at that point that he seemed to give in and demand release. But Jacob, ever the bargainer, refused to let go without a blessing. He got one, including a change of name that meant "power with God and with man." That told him what he had already guessed, that he had been wrestling with God himself. So he named the place Peniel, which meant "face of God."

Putting the scene in a different light, Jacob was not winning the wrestling match at any point, but at the same time that God disabled Jacob, he also declared him the winner. It was not Jacob's cleverness or human strength that gave him the victory, but God's grace. It had always been God, not Jacob, who had prevailed to carry out his will. Jacob got the message, reflected in the double name change, but no immediate change was evident in his life.

Think when this event occurred. He had successfully escaped from Laban, but death at the hands of Esau was a definite and imminent possibility. He retreated back into his fear, and with good reason: "Jacob looked up and there was Esau, coming with his four hundred men" (Gen. 33:1). In panic, Jacob divided his family to protect his favorite wife and son as well as he could, relying on his human wit and strength once again.

The contrast between the two brothers at their meeting is almost comical. Esau kissed and wept, while Jacob and his entire household prostrated themselves and sweated. Jacob's only hope, repeated three times in Genesis 33, was "to find favor in your eyes, my lord" (Gen. 33:8, 10, 15). The *NIV Study Bible*'s footnote to verse 4 provides a useful summary: "All Jacob's fears proved unfounded. God had been at work and had so blessed Esau (v. 9) that he no longer held a grudge against Jacob."

The actual confrontation was infinitely less awful than Jacob had dreaded. Interestingly, his thoughts turned to God, and not just as a ploy to gauge his brother's heart: "They are the children God has graciously given your servant" (Gen. 33:5). In contrast to his earlier claim to God's attention because of his hard toil under Laban, here Jacob put God's favor in its true light: "Please accept the present that was brought to you, for God has been gracious to me and I have all I need" (v. 11). It seems that when he came to the brink of his own ability and realized his true helplessness, Jacob finally internalized the faith of his fathers and made it his own. Significantly, when he got to Shechem, he bought a plot of ground "where he pitched his tent. There he set up an altar and called it El Elohe Israel" (vv. 19–20), which meant "God, the God of Israel." At Peniel God had given Jacob a new name that included his own; now Israel gave God a new name that included his own, too.

These beautiful, personal namings are repeated in Genesis 35, expressive of the coming to full circle of God's and Jacob's covenants. The burying of foreign gods in that chapter also completes a theme, and perhaps can be taken to include Jacob's giving up of his reliance on himself, as well.

> Then God said to Jacob, "Go up to Bethel and settle there, and build an altar there to God, who appeared to you when you were fleeing from your brother Esau."
>
> So Jacob said to his household and to all who were with him, "Get rid of the foreign gods you have with you, and purify yourselves and change your clothes. Then come, let us go up to Bethel, where I will build an altar to God, who answered me in the day of my distress and who has been with me wherever I have gone." . . . There he built an altar, and he called the place El Bethel, because it was there that God revealed himself to him when he was fleeing from his brother." . . .
>
> After Jacob returned from Paddan Aram, God appeared to him again and blessed him. God said to him, "Your name is Jacob, but you will no longer be called Jacob; your name will be Israel." So he named him Israel.
>
> And God said to him, "I am God Almighty; be fruitful and increase in number. A nation and a community of nations will come from you, and kings will come from your body. The land I gave to Abraham and Isaac I also give to you, and I will give this land to your descendants after you." Then God went up from him at the place where he had talked with him.
>
> Jacob set up a stone pillar at the place where God had talked with him, and he poured out a drink offering on it; he also poured oil on it. Jacob called the place where God had talked with him Bethel (Gen. 35:1–14, *passim*).

Shepherding

The repetitive summary above and the listing of Jacob's and Esau's genealogies in Genesis 35 and 36 might make us think this was the end of Jacob's life, but such is not the case. True, the focus switches to the actions of his offspring, particularly Simeon and Levi, Judah, and Joseph, whose special story we will take up in the next study. But we don't want to miss Jacob's final *Henani*, or the wonderful peace that pervaded the end of his life. In going to Egypt and in blessing his sons and grandsons, he manifested total security in the watch-care of his God. Jacob had surrendered himself to the almighty, and so could rest deeply in God's promises, even as he remained open to his surprises.

After Joseph had revealed himself to his brothers, he instructed them to bring Jacob and all their children and grandchildren to Egypt, where he could provide for them out of the storehouses he as overseer had had built and filled.

> So Israel set out with all that was his, and when he reached Beersheba, he offered sacrifices to the God of his father Isaac.
> And God spoke to Israel in a vision at night and said, "Jacob! Jacob!"
> "Here I am [*Henani*]," he replied.
> "I am God, the God of your father," he said. "Do not be afraid to go down to Egypt, for I will make you into a great nation there. I will go down to Egypt with you, and I will surely bring you back again. And Joseph's own hand will close your eyes" (Gen. 46:1–4).

Jacob lived in Egypt seventeen years, and when his time came to die, he was ready. First, he made Joseph swear he would take his bones back to the family cave at Mamre for burial. "Then Joseph swore to him, and Israel worshiped as he leaned on the top of his staff" (Gen. 47:31). The assurance that he would be cared for after death as he had been cared for in life evoked worship from Jacob's heart, and this line is thus a fitting summation of his faith in Hebrews 11.

When Joseph brought his two sons to Jacob's deathbed, Jacob adopted them as his own and blessed them as heads of distinct half-tribes. He also repeated God's promise:

> Jacob said to Joseph, "God Almighty appeared to me at Luz in the land of Canaan, and there he blessed me and said to me, 'I

am going to make you fruitful and will increase your numbers. I
will make you a community of peoples and I will give this land
as an everlasting possession to your descendants after you'"
(Gen. 48:3–4).

Then he blessed Joseph and said,
"May the God before whom my fathers Abraham and Isaac
walked,
the God who has been *my* Shepherd all my life to this day,
the Angel who has delivered *me* from all harm—may he bless
these boys.
May they be called by *my* name and the names of my fathers
Abraham and Isaac,
and may they increase greatly upon the earth" (Gen. 48:15–16,
italics added).

In the next chapter, Jacob gathered his other sons so he could
bless them in turn and "tell you what will happen to you in days
to come" (Gen. 49:1). Not all the prophecy is pleasant, but it is
inspired, and it fit the names and the characters of each of the
tribes that would descend from them. When he came to Joseph,
Jacob again stressed his own identity with the Shepherd:

Joseph is a fruitful vine,
a fruitful vine near a spring, whose branches climb over a wall.
With bitterness archers attacked him; they shot at him with hostility.
But his bow remained steady, his strong arms stayed limber,
because of the hand of the Mighty One of Jacob.
because of the Shepherd, the Rock of Israel.
because of *your father's* God, who helps you,
because of the Almighty, who blesses you
with blessings of the heavens above, blessings of the deep that
lies below,
blessings of the breast and womb.
Your father's blessings are greater than the blessings of the ancient
mountains,
than the bounty of the age-old hills.
Let all these rest on the head of Joseph,
on the brow of the prince among his brothers (Gen. 49:22–26,
italics added).

"When Jacob had finished giving instructions to his sons, he drew his feet up into the bed, breathed his last and was gathered to his people" (Gen. 49:33). He was embalmed and mourned in Egypt, then carried to Canaan for burial as he had made Joseph promise. Four hundred years later, the Israelites, now a whole nation called by Jacob's new name, carried the bones of Joseph out of Egypt with them during the Exodus.

In life and in death, do you have the kind of peace that Jacob found in his God? Coming up against the limitations of his own considerable strength and cunning, he found faith when he faced up to his true condition of helplessness, and saw God face to face. Jacob was a most capable man, whose worldly successes could not bring him the one thing he really wanted—his brother's forgiveness. What is it you really want? Will you give up relying on your own strength to realize your goals, and instead come to worship God in true humility, leaning on the end of your staff, as Jacob did?

> Children of the heavenly Father
> Safely in his bosom gather;
> Nestling bird nor star in heaven
> Such a refuge e'er was given.
>
> God his own doth tend and nourish;
> In his holy courts they flourish.
> From all evil things he spares them;
> In his mighty arms he bears them.
>
> Neither life nor death shall ever
> From the Lord his children sever;
> Unto them his grace he showeth,
> And their sorrows all he knoweth.
>
> Though he giveth or he taketh,
> God his children ne'er forsaketh;
> His the loving purpose solely
> To preserve them pure and holy.
> Carolina Sandell-Berg, 1858
> Trans. by Ernest W. Olson, 1925

6

Joseph
The Serving Self

Primary Scripture Reading

Genesis 29–30; 35:16–20; 37; 39–50

Supplementary References

Luke 22:24–50
Job 13:15
Psalm 56, 84, 118

Questions for Study and Discussion

1. The account of Joseph's life seems to fall into a series of turning points. Fill in the chart on the next page with key words or phrases to highlight the major actions and attitudes of each scene and Joseph's response to it.

2. Recall the sibling rivalry passed down to Joseph and his brothers from their father and grandfather. In what ways are your family patterns repetitions of the past? What thoughts helped to change Joseph's relationship with his brothers? How could his process help you to overcome a similar problem?

3. At what point did Joseph say *Henani,* and to whom? What were both the immediate and ultimate consequences? Describe Joseph's overall feelings throughout all the ups and downs of his life.

4. What had Joseph done to deserve being thrown into prison? How long was he there altogether, do you think? How did he occupy his time? Meanwhile, what did the people around him do? How was Joseph able to keep working and avoid bitterness over his multiple mistreatments?

Verses	Place	Others' Actions/Attitudes	Joseph's Actions/Attitudes
Gen. 29–30	Laban's house	rivalry, favoritism	
Gen. 37	Jacob's house	Father: favors Joseph; sends to brothers	enjoys special favor; goes willingly
	fields	Brothers: resent Joseph; sell Joseph into slavery	surprised at treachery
Gen. 39	Potiphar's	Potiphar: puts Joseph in charge of household	serves; prospers
		Potiphar's wife:	
Gen. 39–40	Prison	Warden:	
		Fellow prisoners:	
Gen. 41–50		Pharaoh:	
		Brothers:	
		Jacob:	

What similarities do you find between incidents in Joseph's life and those related in Psalm 56, 84, and 118?

5. Joseph's period of power had its potential pitfalls, too. Cite Bible texts to show Joseph's constant focus on God rather than on his own brilliance during his administration of Egypt.

6. What insights into the character or methods of God do you discover in connection with Joseph's life? Is there evidence of Joseph speaking to God, or hearing from him directly? What and how did Joseph know about God? How does Joseph's example challenge you?

One of my favorite nursery songs is "The Eensy Weensy Spider." No matter how many times he got washed out by the rain, he always came out with the sun to climb the garden spout again. He never complained, never cried "Why me?" or "Unfair," never gave up, never even thought of packing up his web and trying his luck elsewhere. Weather permitting, he climbed.

Joseph reminds me of that spider. Washed out again and again, rejected, mistreated, forgotten, he kept on climbing. He seemed to have a way of discovering the cherries in each of the pits of misfortune where he found himself. It wasn't just the power of positive thinking that enabled Joseph to maintain his optimism and patience through every adversity. It was his faith in God's perfect control of every situation, whether it seemed good or bad to Joseph at the time, which he always beautifully expressed in an attitude of devoted service to each of the human masters God placed over him.

Joseph was not without resources. He was young, handsome, honest, intelligent, and diligent, and his genuine goodness was recognized by all who saw him, a fact which sometimes created difficulties, as we shall see. But Joseph's greatest resource was God. As we study the ups and downs of his life, we shall always find Joseph praising his God, the giver of life, prosperity, and truth.

71

In the Pit

The familiar Sunday-school lesson of Joseph's betrayal at the hands of his brothers is found in Genesis 37, but to comprehend the whole story we must examine clues from throughout the span of his father's life. "What man learns from history is that man learns nothing from history," said the German philosopher Hegel, and his words can be aptly applied to Jacob. Tasting, as he had, the bitter fruits of parental favoritism and sibling rivalry in relation to his own parents, brother, in-laws, and wives, what did he do but pass on the poison to his own sons. Joseph was set apart by the gift of a "richly ornamented robe," which added painful visual confirmation of what all the brothers knew:

> Now Israel loved Joseph more than any of his other sons, because he had been born to him in his old age; and he made a richly ornamented robe for him. When his brothers saw that their father loved him more than any of them, they hated him and could not speak a kind word to him (Gen. 37:3–4).

Joseph, a young man of seventeen, was no more sensitive to the feelings of other people than are most teenagers. Full of himself, flaunting his special cloak, he added injury to insult by tattling to his father about the way his brothers behaved while they tended the flocks (Gen. 37:2). Perhaps it was only an attempt at morning conversation, and not really pouring salt in the wound, that caused him to repeat his two dreams about his preeminence over his family. Unfortunately, Joseph didn't have the advantage of the completed text, as we do, to see his brothers' building fury:

> Joseph had a dream, and when he told it to his brothers, they hated him all the more. He said to them, "Listen to this dream I had: We were binding sheaves of grain out in the field when suddenly my sheaf rose and stood upright, while your sheaves gathered around mine and bowed down to it."
>
> His brothers said to him, "Do you intend to reign over us? Will you actually rule us?" And they hated him all the more because of his dream and what he had said.

> Then he had another dream, and he told it to his broth-
> ers. . . . When he told his father as well as his brothers, his
> father rebuked him. . . . His brothers were jealous of him, but
> his father kept the matter in mind (Gen. 37:5–11).

It seems that Jacob kept Joseph in hand, as well as in mind,
fearing some reprisals. Instead of going out to tend the flocks
again with his brothers, as he had in verse 2, Joseph stayed at
home until Jacob called for him.

> Now his brothers had gone to graze their father's flocks near
> Shechem, and Israel said to Joseph, "As you know, your broth-
> ers are grazing the flocks near Shechem. Come, I am going to
> send you to them."
> "Very well [Henani]," he replied.
> So he said to him, "Go and see if all is well with your brothers
> and with the flocks, and bring word back to me." Then he sent
> him off from the Valley of Hebron (Gen. 37:12–14).

Jacob was asking for another report, but he was also asking for
trouble in sending Joseph beyond the range of his protection.
Apparently, his retention of Joseph's dreams "in mind" was only
in regard to their possible fulfillment, not to their possible consequences. But his brothers remembered, and made their plans as
soon as they saw his ornamented robe approaching.

> So Joseph went after his brothers and found them near Do-
> than. But they saw him in the distance, and before he reached
> them, they plotted to kill him.
> "Here comes that dreamer!" they said to each other. "Come
> now, let's kill him and throw him into one of these cisterns and
> say that a ferocious animal devoured him. Then we'll see what
> comes of his dreams."
> When Reuben heard this, he tried to rescue him from their
> hands. "Let's not take his life," he said. "Don't shed any blood.
> Throw him into this cistern here in the desert, but don't lay a
> hand on him." Reuben said this to rescue him from them and
> take him back to his father.
> So when Joseph came to his brothers, they stripped him of
> his robe—the richly ornamented robe he was wearing—and

73

they took him and threw him into the cistern. Now the cistern was empty; there was no water in it (Gen. 37:17–24).

Even though there was no water in the cistern, it must have been a shocking and degrading experience for Joseph to be seized by his angry brothers, stripped of his fancy robe, and thrown unceremoniously into the pit. He must also have overheard their nasty arguments against Reuben's plea to spare his life. He tried desperately to make his own appeal, a fact which does not appear in this passage but is referred to by the brothers twenty years later: "Surely we are being punished because of our brother. We saw how distressed he was when he pleaded with us for his life, but we would not listen; that's why this distress has come upon us" (Gen. 42:21).

In our study of Isaac, we considered the profound impression on his mind made by the memory of Abraham's knife at his neck. Here, we see the heavy burden of guilt that weighed on Joseph's brothers for years after their crime, even to the end of their lives, despite his repeated sincere assurances. But somehow, Joseph seemed to escape the lasting inner torment of this most traumatic event. What was his secret for rising above the agonizing reality of his family's mistreatment of him? Perhaps in his example, others who have suffered abuse can find practical support and comfort.

First, let us notice that years later in Egypt, when he revealed himself to his brothers, there is no evidence he harbored resentment. It is true he put them through a rigorous series of tests: he kept his identity a secret, though he recognized his brothers immediately; he spoke to them harshly; and several times he deliberately put them in fear of death by starvation or punishment. Admittedly, there may have been a tinge of satisfaction for Joseph to make his brothers taste their own medicine and experience something of his own anxiety back in the cistern. But in all these trials, his intent was to gauge their loyalty, and his motive was love, not revenge. Each time he saw them, he wept (Gen. 42:24; 43:30; 45:1–2, 14–15; 46:29; and even 50:17), and his forgiveness was complete.

But it was not only hindsight that enabled Joseph to let go of his anger, which was never really pent up in the first place. One avenue of relief to those who have been mistreated is the belief that things have actually turned out all right in the aftermath of the mistreatment, or even better than expected. Joseph had been aware of God's guiding hand throughout his life. Joseph's concern was not for his own feelings but his brothers'; as he hastened to console them.

Joseph said to his brothers, "I am Joseph! Is my father still living?" But his brothers were not able to answer him, because they were terrified at his presence.

Then Joseph said to his brothers, "Come close to me." When they had done so, he said, "I am your brother Joseph, the one you sold into Egypt! And now, do not be distressed and do not be angry with yourselves for selling me here, because it was to save lives that God sent me ahead of you. For two years now there has been famine in the land, and for the next five years there will not be plowing and reaping. But God sent me ahead of you to preserve for you a remnant on earth and to save your lives by a great deliverance (Gen. 45:3–7).

Even long after the Israelites were settled in Goshen following the death of Jacob, Joseph's brothers were still nervous about the possible reversal of Joseph's expressed love.

When Joseph's brothers saw that their father was dead, they said, "What if Joseph holds a grudge against us and pays us back for all the wrongs we did to him?" So they sent word to Joseph, saying, "Your father left these instructions before he died: 'This is what you are to say to Joseph: I ask you to forgive your brothers the sins they committed in treating you so badly.' Now please forgive the sins of the servants of the God of your father." When their message came to him, Joseph wept.

His brothers then came and threw themselves down before him. "We are your slaves," they said.

But Joseph said to them, "Don't be afraid. Am I in the place of God? You intended to harm me, but God intended it for good to accomplish what is now being done, the saving of many lives. So then, don't be afraid. I will provide for you and your children."

And he reassured them and spoke kindly to them (Gen. 50:15–21).

How did Joseph avoid the pitfall of spending the intervening years nursing or mollifying his anger against his brothers, as Esau and others had done? Perhaps it was because he had noticed something important the moment he was thrown into the cistern: "Now the cistern was empty; there was no water in it." When the biblical account of thousands of years is so brief, I always marvel that some seemingly trivial tidbit of information is reiterated. Joseph was aware of God's particular care for him when he hit the dry bottom of the well. He hadn't drowned, or even gotten dirty, and for the moment he was safe from his quarreling brothers. Even being sold to the Ishmaelites was a sort of rescue, and could be looked on as something of a great adventure that this feisty teenager could, and would, someday tell his grandchildren. In every difficult circumstance in his life, and there were many, Joseph kept his mind focused on the fact that he was at least still alive, and he set about to live in thankful service to the God who had saved him and would ultimately save many through him. He didn't have to wait for the happy ending to begin responding to God's call. He didn't say, "Wait a minute, this is not what I imagined my life would be like." He answered, *"Henani,"* immediately, and simply accepted the pits as well as the privileges as different stages in the ongoing plan of God.

In Prosperity and Prison

There are several parallels between Joseph's first experience in the cistern and his imprisonment in pharaoh's dungeon, and the same Hebrew term is used in both cases to indicate his downfall from prestige. But there must have been quite a difference in the physical description of the two places. The prison of Egypt, though obviously a place of confinement, sounds more like our minimum security facility for high-ranking white-collar offenders than a penitentiary or torture chamber for hardened criminals. Clearly, it represented a loss of status for Joseph and the other inmates, but once again it was also a place of protection and continued service.

Another matter connected with Joseph's life at this time concerns the identity of the prison warden. Genesis 39 opens with these words: "Now Joseph had been taken down to Egypt. Potiphar, an Egyptian who was one of Pharaoh's officials, the captain of the guard, bought him from the Ishmaelites who had taken him there" (Gen. 39:1). The *NIV Study Bible* notes that the Hebrew word translated "guard" in Gen. 37:36 can mean either "executioners (the captain of whom was in charge of the royal prisoners)" or "butchers (the captain of whom was the chief cook in the royal court)." If we take it to mean the first type, could it not be that this same Potiphar was the warden in charge of the prison where Joseph was put in custody? We cannot answer this question with certainty, but two other verses give me reason to think it possible. First, in Genesis 40:2–3 we read, "Pharaoh was angry with his two officials, the chief cupbearer and the chief baker, and put them in custody in the house of the captain of the guard, in the same prison where Joseph was confined. The captain of the guard assigned them to Joseph, and he attended them."

The second clue to the identity of the jailer lies in the behavior of Potiphar in Genesis 39: "When his master heard the story his wife told him, saying, 'This is how your slave treated me,' he burned with anger. Joseph's master took him and put him in prison, the place where the king's prisoners were confined" (Gen. 39:19–20). Here the *NIV Study Bible* notes, "Though understandably angry (see v. 19), Potiphar put Joseph in the 'house of the captain of the guard' (40:3)—certainly not the worst prison available."

Have you wondered why Potiphar didn't have Joseph at least flogged, if not mutilated or murdered? Against whom did his anger burn? Against Joseph for violating his wife, or against his wife for making an outrageous claim that cost him the services of such an excellent steward? If he were in fact the same man who was in charge of the king's prisoners, he could have solved his dilemma by simply transferring Joseph from the private to the public sector of management.

Some additional support for this possibility may be found in the fact that a similar phrase is used to describe both Potiphar's and the warden's appraisal of Joseph: "The warden paid no attention to anything under Joseph's care, because the LORD was with Joseph and gave him success in whatever he did" (Gen. 39:23). Joseph had served Potiphar with the same conscientious attention to detail. His devotion to his master's well-being was more than noteworthy; the prosperity that accompanied Joseph in all that he did was truly remarkable, so much so that it was reiterated five times in one paragraph:

> The LORD was with Joseph and he prospered, and he lived in the house of his Egyptian master. When his master saw that the LORD was with him and that the LORD gave him success in every-thing he did, Joseph found favor in his eyes and became his attendant. Potiphar put him in charge of his household, and he entrusted to his care everything he owned. From the time he put him in charge of his household and of all that he owned, the LORD blessed the household of the Egyptian because of Joseph. The blessing of the LORD was on everything Potiphar had, both in the house and in the field. So he left in Joseph's care every-thing he had; with Joseph in charge, he did not concern himself with anything except the food he ate (Gen. 39:2–6).

Notice the causal sequence of events. The blessing and pros-perity connected with Joseph attracted Potiphar's attention. Joseph found favor in his sight, and was entrusted with more and more responsibility, while Potiphar concerned himself with less and less. But Joseph never became cocky about his position or the true source of his success. In every sentence, God's role is stressed: "The LORD was with Joseph . . . . the LORD was with him . . . . the LORD gave him success . . . . the LORD blessed the household of the Egyptian because of Joseph . . . . the blessing of the LORD was on everything. . . ."

God's hand was on Joseph's life for more than to bestow blessing. Not only did it keep him humble and grateful for all his benefits, but it also kept him from evil. When Potiphar's wife cast her eye in Joseph's direction as an object of seduction, two things saved him: his focus on God and his swift feet. He said,

With me in charge, my master does not concern himself with anything in the house; everything he owns he has entrusted to my care. No one is greater in this house than I am. My master has withheld nothing from me except you, because you are his wife. How then could I do such a wicked thing and sin against God? (Gen. 39:8–9).

Then he put distance between himself and temptation. He "refused to go to bed with her or even be with her" (Gen. 39:10). Finally, "he left his cloak in her hand and ran out of the house" (Gen. 39:12).

Joseph did not escape altogether the consequences of her evil. He was still falsely accused and thrown into prison, even though he was completely innocent. So how did he manage to avoid the traps of bitterness and discouragement that seem to beset us so often? Joseph was always aware that the same Lord was with him everywhere, here in the prison as well as when he had been in the pit or in Potiphar's house, so that he had no reason to cease praising and serving him. He refused to indulge in self-pity and instead turned his full attention to the needs of those placed in his care. And it was precisely through this sensitivity to the other inmates that Joseph's way of escape was eventually to come. God was still his provider and protector, and until such time as he would arrange another change, there was work to be done.

There is one more line to consider before we move on with Joseph. We don't know exactly how long he served in Potiphar's house, nor how long he was in prison before he met the chief baker and cupbearer, but we sense the slow passage of time while Joseph waited for deliverance: "The chief cupbearer, however, *did not remember* Joseph; he *forgot* him" (Gen. 40:23–41:1, italics added) for two full years, in fact. It is easy for us to nod knowingly and say, "Isn't that just the way with people? Ungrateful!" What is more important to notice is that God never forgot Joseph for one moment, nor does he forget his children today.

> I lift up my eyes to the hills—where does my help come from?
> My help comes from the LORD, the Maker of heaven and earth.
>
> He will not let your foot slip—he who watches over you will not slumber;
> indeed, he who watches over Israel will neither slumber nor sleep.
>
> The LORD watches over you—the LORD is your shade at your right hand;
> the sun will not harm you by day, nor the moon by night.
>
> The LORD will keep you from all harm—he will watch over your life,
> the LORD will watch over your coming and going, both now and forevermore (Ps. 121).

While God worked in all of nature, controlling climate and crops to orchestrate the movements of entire nations, he continued to season Joseph for the highest level of service. Can you believe the truth of God's constant care, as Joseph did, even when you feel forgotten and unappreciated by others? And while you wait eagerly for deliverance from your real and painful prison, will you praise your Lord for the prosperity and protection he provides?

In Power

Joseph's final upward climb, from prison to high position in Egypt, shows us still other aspects of God's character to which we can cling in our distress. If we can concentrate on God's complete control over time, and on his essential nature as the embodiment of truth, we have no need to despair. Let us look to the end of Joseph's story for these lessons.

The way out of Joseph's last pit was once again through the grace and gift of God. We were introduced to the theme of dreams early in his life, when he told his brothers that he had seen their sheaves of grain and their stars bow down before him

(Gen. 37:7–9), and we can follow it throughout his life. Although he may have sounded boastful at first, he quickly learned to keep quiet about what God revealed to him when he experienced his brothers' violent reaction. By the time the prophecy was fulfilled, his attitude had changed. No longer an impulsive teenager, Joseph used his gifts of interpretation to comfort others and offer insight into God's plans. It was not for his own greatness that he had been given this power, but for God's glory, and Joseph was careful to praise him for his truth.

> After they had been in custody for some time, each of the two men—the cupbearer and the baker of the king of Egypt, who were being held in prison—had a dream the same night, and each dream had a meaning of its own.
> When Joseph came to them the next morning, he saw that they were dejected. So he asked Pharaoh's officials who were in custody with him in his master's house, "Why are your faces so sad today?"
> "We both had dreams," they answered, "but there is no one to interpret them."
> Then Joseph said to them, "Do not interpretations belong to God? Tell me your dreams" (Gen. 40:4–8).

Joseph gave straightforward explanations of the meanings of the dreams as God revealed them to him. He did not use his talent simply to give false hope or to win friends or favor. "When the chief baker saw that Joseph had given a favorable interpretation, he said to Joseph, 'I too had a dream'" (Gen. 40:16), expecting an equally favorable reply. Unfortunately, the meaning of his dream was horrible, all the more so because it came to pass in every detail.

Although two years were to pass before the incident came back into his mind, the chief cupbearer had been impressed by both the honesty and the accuracy of Joseph's interpretations. He said to the troubled pharaoh, "We told him our dreams, and he interpreted them for us, giving each man the interpretation of his dream. And things turned out exactly as he interpreted them to us: I was restored to my position, and the other man was hanged" (Gen. 41:12–13).

The most interesting exchange occurred between the august pharaoh and Joseph, when the latter was summoned to clean himself up and present himself at court.

> Pharaoh said to Joseph, "I had a dream, and no one can interpret it. But I have heard it said of you that when you hear a dream you can interpret it."
>
> "I cannot do it," Joseph replied to Pharaoh, "but God will give Pharaoh the answer he desires" (Gen. 41:15–16).

It was not a moment for Joseph to be splitting hairs with pharaoh over who was or was not able to reveal the meaning of his dreams. Not one of the magicians in Egypt had been able to solve the puzzle by any power. But the distinction was of crucial importance to Joseph, and throughout their conversation he was careful to stress the authority and the purpose of God:

> Then Joseph said to Pharaoh, "The dreams of Pharaoh are one and the same. God has revealed to Pharaoh what he is about to do. . . . It is just as I said to Pharaoh; God has shown Pharaoh what he is about to do. . . . The reason the dream was given to Pharaoh in two forms is that the matter has been firmly decided by God, and God will do it soon. . . .
>
> The plan seemed good to Pharaoh and to all his officials. So Pharaoh asked them, "Can we find anyone like this man, one in whom is the spirit of God?"
>
> Then Pharaoh said to Joseph, "Since God has made all this known to you, there is no one so discerning and wise as you. You shall be in charge of my palace, and all my people are to submit to your orders. Only with respect to the throne will I be greater than you" (Gen. 41:25–32, 37–40).

Even as Joseph was elevated to high rank in Egypt, he never spoke lightly of the arduous path by which he had come, nor did he ever attribute his success to his own ability or achievement. He accepted all of the pharaoh's gifts as signs of favor and power, and he devoted his own talents to the enormous task of collecting and distributing food. But he always remembered that it was God who had preserved him for a purpose. He named his offspring with this thought: "Joseph named his firstborn Manasseh and said, 'It is because God has made me forget all my trouble and all my father's household.' The second son he named Ephraim and said, 'It is because God has made me fruitful in the land of my suffering'" (Gen. 41:51–52).

Notice that Joseph mentioned his trouble and suffering at the same time as he talked about God. Clearly, this did not seem like a contradiction to him. Bad things had happened, and God brought good things out of them. Joseph made no attempt to repress his past, nor to glorify it, but he did try to maintain a long view of his life, to find meaning in all that had occurred. Seventy years after bringing his brothers to Egypt, he spoke to them about the future in the context of promises made long in the past to their ancestors:

> Then Joseph said to his brothers, "I am about to die. But God will surely come to your aid and take you up out of this land to the land he promised on oath to Abraham, Isaac and Jacob." And Joseph made the sons of Israel swear an oath and said, "God will surely come to your aid, and then you must carry my bones up from this place" (Gen. 50:24–25).

It was for these forward-focused words that Joseph was recognized as a witness to all believers: "By faith Joseph, when his end was near, spoke about the exodus of the Israelites from Egypt and gave instructions about his bones" (Heb. 11:22).

To Joseph, understanding about the past and the future was more than mere passive acquiescence. Thus, when he was reconciled to his brothers, it was not simply with a shrugged "Let bygones be bygones." There were great principles to be grasped, and Joseph insisted that his brothers get the message. Although they had acted out of ignorance, envy, and malice, God had overruled their evil deed to accomplish a great purpose. "And Joseph said unto them, 'Fear not: for am I in the place of God? But as for you, ye thought evil against me; but God meant it unto good, to bring to pass, as it is this day, to save much people alive'" (Gen. 50:19–20 KJV).

Joseph stood in joyful awe before such an almighty God. It was more than a philosophical posture. Joseph's attitude enabled him to love and forgive his brothers for their treachery, to devote himself to the success of his oppressors, to resist temptation, to use his gift of interpretation to help others, to endure disappointment, to be a wise steward, to get the most out of both the high and low experiences of his life. Consider all that Joseph learned about the character of God: his omnipresence, even in the pit and in prison; his omnipotence, providing abundance and blessing even to the households of foreign masters; and his omniscience, revealing and accomplishing his will according to his perfect plan for all humankind.

What lessons from Joseph's life can you apply to your situation? Perhaps you have suffered physical or psychological abuse. If so, don't try vainly to bury it. Instead, build on it. Look to God to develop a more purposeful perspective on your troubles, and a more positive outlook as you seek to serve others while waiting upon him. In the ups and downs of your life, it may well rain again, but you can choose to keep climbing.

> Come, thou fount of every blessing, tune my heart to sing thy grace;
> Streams of mercy, never ceasing, call for songs of loudest praise.
> Teach me some melodious sonnet, sung by flaming tongues above;
> Praise his name—I'm fixed upon it—Name of God's redeeming love.
>
> Hitherto thy love has blest me; thou hast brought me to this place;
> And I know thy hand will bring me safely home by thy good grace.
> Jesus sought me when a stranger, wandering from the fold of God;
> He, to rescue me from danger, bought me with his precious blood.
>
> O to grace how great a debtor daily I'm constrained to be!
> Let Thy goodness, like a fetter, bind my wandering heart to thee:

Prone to wander, Lord, I feel it, prone to leave the God I love;
Here's my heart, O take and seal it; seal it for the courts above.
   Amen.

Robert Robinson, 1758
Adapted by E. Margaret Clarkson, 1973

7

Moses
The Smallness of Self

Primary Scripture Readings

Exodus 1–15
Numbers 12, 16–17, 20
Deuteronomy 30–34

Supplementary References

Psalm 90
Acts 7:17–44
1 Corinthians 13

2 Corinthians 4:7
Hebrews 11:23–29
Revelation 22

Questions for Study and Discussion

1. Identify the members of Moses' family. Who was responsible for his upbringing? What influence did she have on his later life? Describe Moses' relationship with his sister and brother.

2. Why did Moses leave Egypt? How long was he gone? Why did he return? Why was Moses afraid, as related in Exodus 2? Why, in Exodus 3? What lessons or changes had to occur before God could use him as a deliverer of his people? How is God training you? For what? How long is it taking?

3. Beginning in Exodus 3–4 and following, note the highlights in Moses' life and the development of friendship between Moses and God. List Moses' strengths and weaknesses in two separate columns. How are they related?

4. Moses is described as the meekest man on earth. What does "meekness" mean to you? What did Christ think of meekness? Would anyone think of you as meek? Do you? What impressions do you get of Moses from the New Testament passages listed above?

5. Why was Moses denied entrance into the Promised Land? Had he lost his meekness? What warnings and encouragements can you apply to your life from Moses' example?

6. Exodus 15, Psalm 90, and Deuteronomy 32 are songs of Moses. What attributes of God does Moses celebrate? What phrases do you find particularly meaningful? How does Moses express the smallness of personal self in view of God's greatness? Perhaps you would like to compose a song of praise to God.

M oses ranks among the greatest men in history, yet he is called the "meekest man on earth" (Num. 12:3 KJV). As we examine Moses' life, it should not be our desire to put ourselves on his level. Aaron and Miriam in the Old Testament, and Peter, James, and John in the New Testament were reprimanded for such familiarity. What we do want to imitate is his determination to focus on God's greatness, which gave Moses' life its direction and significance. Three phrases summarize the key aspects of Moses' interaction with God Almighty: he hid his face, he fell on his face, and he talked with God face to face.

Face Hidden

Although the first section of the Bible is known as the Five Books of Moses, in recognition of his authorship, Moses' personal history does not begin until the second book, Exodus. The paranoid pharaoh who ruled Egypt at that time had decreed that all Hebrew male infants must be destroyed at birth. Instead, Moses' mother, Jochebed, hid her son in a basket by the river's edge and set his sister Miriam to watch. The pharaoh's daughter soon discovered him and placed him back in his mother's care until he was weaned, when he came to live in the pharaoh's palace. Thus, "Moses was educated in all the wisdom of the Egyptians and was powerful in speech and action" (Acts 7:22). Yet he did not despise his Hebrew heritage; rather, he so identified with the suffering of his people that he killed an Egyptian who was mistreating them. The writer of the Book of Hebrews gives this summary of the first eighty years of Moses' life:

By faith Moses, when he had grown up, refused to be known as the son of Pharaoh's daughter. He chose to be mistreated along with the people of God rather than to enjoy the pleasures of sin for a short time. He regarded disgrace for the sake of Christ as of greater value than the treasures of Egypt, because he was looking ahead to his reward. By faith he left Egypt, not fearing the king's anger; he persevered because he saw him who is invisible (Heb. 11:24–27).

The text in Exodus 2 records these events and attitudes in detail:

One day, after Moses had grown up, he went out to where his own people were and watched them at their hard labor. He saw an Egyptian beating a Hebrew, one of his own people. Glancing this way and that and seeing no one, he killed the Egyptian and hid him in the sand. The next day he went out and saw two Hebrews fighting. He asked the one in the wrong, "Why are you hitting your fellow Hebrew?"

The man said, "Who made you ruler and judge over us? Are you thinking of killing me as you killed the Egyptian?" Then Moses was afraid and thought, "What I did must have become known."

When Pharaoh heard of this he tried to kill Moses, but Moses fled from Pharaoh and went to live in Midian, where he sat down by a well (Exod. 2:11–15).

Several insights may be gleaned from this passage. First, Moses felt close kinship with the suffering Hebrews, "his own people," but they were less than willing to accept his offers of help. To them he was at best an outsider, if not a downright traitor, by reason of his having grown up at the Egyptian court. (The feeling on the part of the Israelites that Moses wasn't quite one of them was a factor in their reluctance to accept his leadership throughout the wilderness period.) On the other hand, this incident woke pharaoh to the fact that Moses was a potential threat: if he came to the defense of one Hebrew slave, he might well lead a full-scale rebellion at any time. Moses was justified in his fear and subsequent flight from Egypt. Forty years were to pass before this pharaoh died and God responded to the cry of his covenant people (Exod. 2:23–25).

Moses showed fear, first in "glancing this way and that," in committing murder, and then in hiding the body of the Egyptian. When the two Hebrews taunted him with his deed, he was again afraid. But in his decision to flee Egypt and settle in Midian, he acted sensibly to save his life. His meekness was not synonymous with timidity. He protected the daughters of Reuel/ Jethro from harrassment by shepherds (Exod. 2:16—3:1), and became a shepherd himself, a vocation that required strength and courage. Alone on the far side of the desert forty years later, he responded to the miraculous burning bush with simple curiosity, not fear:

> . . . he led the flock to the far side of the desert and came to Horeb, the mountain of God. There the angel of the LORD appeared to him in flames of fire from within a bush. Moses saw that though the bush was on fire it did not burn up. So Moses thought, "I will go over and see this strange sight—why the bush does not burn up."
>
> When the LORD saw that he had gone over to look, God called to him from within the bush, "Moses, Moses!"
>
> And Moses said, "Here I am [*Henani*]."
>
> "Do not come any closer," God said. "Take off your sandals, for the place where you are standing is holy ground." Then he said, "I am the God of your father, the God of Abraham, the God of Isaac and the God of Jacob." At this, Moses hid his face, because he was afraid to look at God (Exod. 3:1–6).

In our study of Adam, we considered hiding from God an indication of shame, resulting from sin. But here, Moses' hidden face underscored the awesome brightness of the presence of God, on whom no one can look and live (Exod. 33:20).

The above passage also includes Moses' *Henani* response to God's initial call. More conversations are recorded between God and Moses than between any other persons in the Bible. Always the greatness of God is emphasized, along with the humility, or meekness, of Moses' approach to God on behalf of his people. Moses yielded himself in service to God, but he had grave doubts about his own qualifications for service. As soon as he heard God's plan, he expressed his personal misgivings, which he reiterated over the next several chapters.

> [God said] ". . . And now the cry of the Israelites has reached me, and I have seen the way the Egyptians are oppressing them. So now, go. I am sending you to Pharaoh to bring my people the Israelites out of Egypt."
>
> But Moses said to God, "Who am I, that I should go to Pharaoh and bring the Israelites out of Egypt?"
>
> And God said, "I will be with you. And this will be the sign to you that it is I who have sent you: When you have brought the people out of Egypt, you will worship God on this mountain" (Exod. 3:9–12).

Moses' "Here am I" quickly became "Who am I?" when he realized the magnitude of the task, the haughtiness of the people to whom he was being sent (based on his own experience of rejection), and his own inadequacy. God's assurance of his presence was not immediately perceived by Moses to be the fulfillment of his need. Moses asked for details and signs to cover a variety of hypothetical cases: "Suppose I go to the Israelites and say to them, 'The God of your fathers has sent me to you,' and they ask me, 'What is his name?' Then what shall I tell them?" (Exod. 3:13); "What if they do not believe me or listen to me and say, 'The LORD did not appear to you'?" (Exod. 4:1). Even when God answered these objections with provisions, still

> Moses said to the LORD, "O Lord, I have never been eloquent, neither in the past nor since you have spoken to your servant. I am slow of speech and tongue."
>
> The LORD said to him, "Who gave man his mouth? Who makes him deaf or dumb? Who gives him sight or makes him blind? Is it not I, the LORD? Now go; I will help you speak and will teach you what to say."
>
> But Moses said, "O Lord, please send someone else to do it."
>
> Then the LORD's anger burned against Moses and he said, "What about your brother, Aaron the Levite? I know he can speak well. He is already on his way to meet you, and his heart will be glad when he sees you. You shall speak to him and put words in his mouth; I will help both of you speak and will teach

you what to do. He will speak to the people for you, and it will be as if he were your mouth and as if you were God to him. But take this staff in your hand so you can perform miraculous signs with it" (Exod. 4:10–17).

Two chapters later, Moses was still unconvinced that God had chosen well.

Now when the LORD spoke to Moses in Egypt, he said to him, "I am the LORD. Tell Pharaoh king of Egypt everything I tell you."

But Moses said to the LORD, "Since I speak with faltering lips, why would Pharaoh listen to me?"

Then the LORD said to Moses, "See, I have made you like God to Pharaoh, and your brother will be your prophet. You are to say everything I command you, and your brother Aaron is to tell Pharaoh to let the Israelites go out of his country. But I will harden Pharaoh's heart, and though I multiply my miraculous signs and wonders in Egypt, he will not listen to you. Then *I* will lay *my* hand on Egypt and with mighty acts of judgment *I* will bring out *my* divisions, *my* people the Israelites. And the Egyptians will know that *I* am the LORD when *I* stretch out *my* hand against Egypt and bring the Israelites out of it" (Exod. 6:28—7:5, italics added).

As we found in our study of other patriarchs, we see again that God knows the weaknesses of his creatures and promises his perfection and strength to perform his will when we are willing. When we refuse to avail ourselves of such a privileged partnership, we are likely to incur his displeasure and risk his selection of other servants to accomplish his work. Perhaps Moses' perceived disabilities—his age, his alien status, and whatever physical handicaps he may have had—were in fact the very reasons he was chosen, that God's own glory might be made known in all the earth (2 Cor. 4:7). Moses was successful as long as he attributed all success to God alone; his downfall occurred when he forgot his essential inadequacy and the unique source of all his power.

The greatness of God is the focus of two songs of Moses,

recorded in Exodus 15 and Psalm 90, rich expressions of action and praise. Notice how Moses extolled God both for his general attributes and for his specific acts:

> . . . he is highly exalted. The horse and its rider he has hurled into the sea. The LORD is my strength and my song; he has become my salvation. . . . Your right hand, O LORD, was majestic in power. . . . In the greatness of your majesty you threw down those who opposed you. . . . Who among the gods is like you, O LORD? Who is like you—majestic in holiness, awesome in glory, working wonders? . . . In your unfailing love you will lead the people you have redeemed. In your strength you will guide them to your holy dwelling. . . . The LORD will reign for ever and ever" (Exod. 15:1–18, *passim*).

> Lord, you have been our dwelling place throughout all generations . . . from everlasting to everlasting you are God. . . . For a thousand years in your sight are like a day that has just gone by, or like a watch in the night. . . . Who knows the power of your anger? For your wrath is as great as the fear that is due you. Teach us to number our days aright, that we may gain a heart of wisdom. . . . Satisfy us in the morning with your unfailing love, that we may sing for joy and be glad all our days. . . . May your deeds be shown to your servants, your splendor to their children" (Ps. 90).

Moses contrasted God's infinity and eternity with our human frailty—our lives are like grass, withered in a day, as opposed to the massive mountains God has made. We can do nothing in our own strength, and he could wipe us out with a mere gesture or thought, yet he acts to help us against our enemies, to save us by his love. What a great God indeed! How do you measure yourself compared with him?

Remember that God's personal call to you does not ascribe any greatness to you at all. You are neither promoted nor perfected in any way. When we by faith accept his offer of cleansing by the blood of Christ, it is Christ's glory that increases, and that he renders back to the Father. To be great in service to God means to accept our own smallness without either frustration or pride.

Moses' protest of inadequacy did not come as news to God.
What angered him was Moses' refusal of God's more-than-ade-
quate capacity to perform the task. When he gives you a job, it is
an expression of ingratitude and false modesty to back away
from such an opportunity and apologize by saying, "Sorry, I'm
just not good enough to be of use." God persevered and persuaded Moses to prove to all Israel that he alone was sufficient.
The Feast of Passover was established to celebrate the power of
his mighty arm and outstretched hand to deliver his people, not
because of their merits, but because of God's mercy. Likewise,
our response of willing humility is entirely appropriate, and all
that he expects. The question, Who am I, that you should send
me? is unnecessary. Knowing the answer to the better question,
Who are you, Lord, that you should call me? enables each feeble
creature to proceed with confidence, not in ourselves, but in
him.

Face Downward

Moses hid his face because he was afraid to look at God, and
rightly so. But he was not afraid to speak to him, expressing his
fears and problems. An experienced shepherd after forty years
in Midian, Moses already understood the nature of the human
flock God now gave him. The question put to him by the
Hebrew in Egypt, "Who made you ruler and judge over us?"
(Exod. 2:14), had not been forgotten, and Moses knew he
needed proof that God had indeed sent him back to Egypt as
ruler, judge, and deliverer of his people. God equipped him
with both words and visible evidence, establishing his authority
for the benefit of the Israelites, of the current pharaoh, and of his
own peace.

> God said to Moses, "I AM WHO I AM. This is what you are to
> say to the Israelites: 'I AM has sent me to you.'
> God also said to Moses, "Say to the Israelites, 'The LORD, the
> God of your fathers—the God of Abraham, the God of Isaac and
> the God of Jacob—has sent me to you.' This is my name by
> which I am to be remembered from generation to genera-
> tion. . . .

The elders of Israel will listen to you. Then you and the elders are to go to the king of Egypt and say to him, 'The LORD, the God of the Hebrews, has met with us. . . .' But I know that the king of Egypt will not let you go unless a mighty hand compels him. So I will stretch out my hand and strike the Egyptians with all the wonders that I will perform among them. After that, he will let you go" (Exod. 3:14–20).

God also gave Moses three signs: the turning of his shepherd's staff into a snake, the turning of his hand white with leprosy and then clean again, and the turning of the Nile water into blood. (Exod. 4:1–9). These miracles encapsulated God's power to make the dead come to life and the living dead. When shown to the Israelites, these signs led them to faith:

Then Moses told Aaron everything the LORD had sent him to say, and also about all the miraculous signs he had commanded him to perform.

Moses and Aaron brought together all the elders of the Israelites, and Aaron told them everything the LORD had said to Moses. He also performed the signs before the people, and they believed. And when they heard that the LORD was concerned about them and had seen their misery, they bowed down and worshiped (Exod. 4:28–31).

Moses became shepherd of Israel with a flock of one million souls, an enormous responsibility. But leading them out of Egypt, feeding and clothing them for forty years in the desert, and settling their disputes were not his biggest worries. These were taken care of by God himself, who performed many miracles to protect them from their enemies (Exod. 14:21–28; 17:8–16), guide them in the wilderness (Exod. 13:20–22), provide food and water (Exod. 16, 17:1–7), and even keep their clothes from wearing out (Deut. 8:4). The institution of an effective judicial system alleviated some of Moses' decision-making responsibilities (Exod. 18:13–26).

What concerned Moses most was not the physical needs so much as the spiritual state of his people. He knew them to be proud and disobedient—traits intolerable to God. It was on their account that he prostrated himself when he saw and heard the Lord on Mount Sinai.

> The the LORD came down in the cloud and stood there with him and proclaimed his name, the LORD. And he passed in front of Moses, proclaiming, "The LORD, the LORD, the compassionate and gracious God, slow to anger, abounding in love and faithfulness, maintaining love to thousands, and forgiving wickedness, rebellion and sin. Yet he does not leave the guilty unpunished; he punishes the children and their children for the sin of the fathers to the third and fourth generation."
> Moses bowed to the ground at once and worshiped. "O Lord, if I have found favor in your eyes," he said, "then let the Lord go with us. Although this is a stiff-necked people, forgive our wickedness and our sin, and take us as your inheritance" (Exod. 34:5–9).

Later, when the priesthood and the sacrifices were instituted, the Israelites joined him in this prone position.

> Then Aaron lifted his hands toward the people and blessed them. And having sacrificed the sin offering, the burnt offering and the fellowship offering, he stepped down.
> Moses and Aaron then went into the Tent of Meeting. When they came out, they blessed the people; and the glory of the LORD appeared to all the people. Fire came out from the presence of the LORD and consumed the burnt offering and the fat portions on the altar. And when all the people saw it, they shouted for joy and fell facedown (Lev. 9:22–24).

The glory of God brought the people to their knees. His holiness was a call to consecration: "I am the LORD your God; consecrate yourselves and be holy, because I am holy. . . . I am the LORD who brought you up out of Egypt to be your God; therefore be holy, because I am holy" (Lev. 11:44–45).

But the command and the performance were not the same thing. Again and again, Moses as their leader fell face downward before the Lord in intercessory prayer for his rebellious people when they grumbled against him and against God. In Numbers 14, all the Israelites responded with fear to the report of giants in Canaan, and voted to return to Egypt. Moses and Aaron fell face downward in front of the whole nation (Num. 14:5). Only Joshua and Caleb urged the people to go on in faith, but the majority talked of stoning the leaders.

> The LORD said to Moses, "How long will these people treat me with contempt? How long will they refuse to believe in me, in spite of all the miraculous signs I have performed among them? I will strike them down with a plague and destroy them, but I will make you into a nation greater and stronger than they."
>
> Moses said to the LORD, "Then the Egyptians will hear about it! By your power you brought these people up from among them. And they will tell the inhabitants of this land about it. They have already heard that you, O LORD, are with these people and that you, O LORD, have been seen face to face, that your cloud stays over them, and that you go before them in a pillar of cloud by day and a pillar of fire by night. If you put these people to death all at one time, the nations who have heard this report about you will say, 'The LORD was not able to bring these people into the land he promised them on oath; so he slaughtered them in the desert.' . . . In accordance with your great love, forgive the sin of these people, just as you have pardoned them from the time they left Egypt until now" (Num. 14:11–19).

Moses fell face downward three more times in Numbers 16, when three men rose up in rebellion against him, and God threatened to wipe out the entire assembly. By his quick appeal and Aaron's atoning sacrifice, only 250 were killed when the earth swallowed up the rebels, and 14,700 more died from a plague in the wake of God's wrath. Still, most of the nation was spared.

Falling face downward before the Lord on behalf of his people signified Moses' role as shepherd-deliverer of Israel. A holy God demanded the punishment of a sinful people, but a compassionate God responded to the leader's appeal for forgiveness. His wrath could be turned aside. Yet, for Moses, letting go of anger was more difficult, and tension built up over his years in the wilderness. The people's rebelliousness wore him down; he took their defiance of God personally. The breaking point came at Meribah.

> Now there was no water for the community, and the people gathered in opposition to Moses and Aaron. . . .
>
> Moses and Aaron went from the assembly to the entrance to the Tent of Meeting and fell facedown, and the glory of the LORD appeared to them. The LORD said to Moses, "Take the staff, and you and your brother Aaron gather the assembly together. Speak to that rock before their eyes and it will pour out its water. You will bring water out of the rock for the community so they and their livestock can drink."
>
> So Moses took the staff from the LORD's presence, just as he commanded him. He and Aaron gathered the assembly together in front of the rock and Moses said to them, "Listen, you rebels, must we bring you water out of this rock?" Then Moses raised his arm and struck the rock twice with his staff. Water gushed out, and the community and their livestock drank.
>
> But the LORD said to Moses and Aaron, "Because you did not trust in me enough to honor me as holy in the sight of the Israelites, you will not bring this community into the land I give them."
>
> These were the waters of Meribah, where the Israelites quarreled with the LORD and where he showed himself holy among them (Num. 20:2–13).

This pivotal passage indicates to what extent Moses' attitude had deteriorated. His anger against the people caused him to reinterpret God's directions, changing the command and putting himself in God's place as provider for their need ("must *we*?"). It was not merely a minor slipup for which he was excluded from entrance into the Promised Land, but rather the sins of arrogance and disobedience at the core of his words. He had failed in his role of shepherd by sinking to the same level of complaining self-centeredness the people had demonstrated all along. He was no longer fit to lead.

What a warning for our lives, if God has called us to both serve and to lead! The role of shepherd—for a flock consisting of a single friend or a family, a congregation or an entire community—is a very important and difficult task. Only God can enable and equip us to serve by faith, without either succumbing to frustration or trying to bask in his glory. It requires both strength and humility to fall face downward before the Lord in fervent prayer. When did you last come to him on your knees on behalf of your wayward followers?

In spite of his failure, Moses retained a unique place on God's honor role: he was permitted to view Canaan from a mountaintop, and when he died, God himself buried him in an unknown grave (Deut. 34:1–6). Throughout the Bible, Moses is represented as God's special friend, who received and recorded his law and upheld his offer of life to those who chose to obey his commands.

Face to Face

God told Moses no one could look at his face and live (Exod. 33:20). When he displayed his glory on Mount Sinai, he carefully shielded Moses from the full blast of his radiance. Even so, Moses' face remained aglow from that exposure, "because he had spoken with the LORD" (Exod. 34:29). From that time on, he kept a veil over his face whenever he spoke to the people, to calm their fear of his strangeness, but he removed it "whenever he entered the LORD's presence to speak with him" (Exod. 34:33–34). After many experiences with God's combined holiness and wrath, the Israelites were even more terrified, and cried to Moses, "We will die! We are lost, we are all lost! Anyone who even comes near the tabernacle of the LORD will die. Are we all going to die?" (Num. 17:12–13). Truly, a holy God is unapproachable to a sinful people, and we have no hope.

Yet the Bible also states specifically that God and Moses had frequent direct communication: "Whenever the people saw the pillar of cloud standing at the entrance to the tent, they all stood and worshiped, each at the entrance to his tent. The LORD would speak to Moses face to face, as a man speaks with his friend" (Exod. 33:10–11). God punished Miriam and Aaron for presuming to enjoy a similar relationship.

> Miriam and Aaron began to talk against Moses because of his Cushite wife, for he had married a Cushite. "Has the LORD spoken only through Moses?" they asked. "Hasn't he also spoken through us?" And the LORD heard this.
>
> (Now Moses was a very humble man, more humble than anyone else on the face of the earth.)
>
> At once the LORD said to Moses, Aaron and Miriam, "Come out to the Tent of Meeting, all three of you." So the three of them came out. Then the LORD came down in a pillar of cloud; he stood at the entrance to the Tent and summoned Aaron and Miriam. When both of them stepped forward, he said, "Listen to my words:

> > "When a prophet of the LORD is among you,
> >   I reveal myself to him in visions,
> >   I speak to him in dreams.
> > But this is not true of my servant Moses;
> >   he is faithful in all my house.
> > With him I speak face to face,
> >   clearly and not in riddles;
> >   he sees the form of the LORD.

> Why then were you not afraid to speak against my servant Moses?" (Num. 12:1–8).

There are several questions of interest here. Did Moses really see God face to face, and if so, why is he the only one who ever did? Or can others do so, also? And what qualifies a person to deserve, and then survive, such an honor?

To the first question, I think the answer must be affirmative. Even though God stated that it couldn't be done, several other passages indicate that Moses in fact was engaged in an ongoing, direct dialogue with the Lord, which also involved his physical presence. When John wrote in the New Testament, "No one has ever seen God, but God the only Son, who is at the Father's side, has made him known" (John 1:18), he was not contradicting the

Scriptures but rather indicating that Moses' interviews were with the second person of the Godhead.

The second issue is more significant for us. God does invite us into his presence today, not to destroy but to save us, and we are accepted because of the atoning sacrifice of Jesus Christ. We can never qualify for his least notice, not to mention for adoption into his family, except by claiming the blood of his own Son, the worthy Lamb, for our protection. If you have taken this step by faith, you can come freely into his presence to worship and to pray for yourself and others. "We have been made holy through the sacrifice of the body of Jesus Christ once for all" (Heb. 10:10). We can come before our holy God without fear of rejection or destruction. But we still need humbly to fall down before him, in adoration and supplication. It is not the dread of what he might do to us, but the awe at what he has already done for us, that should yet cause us to tremble.

But even this accessibility is not the end of what God promises. The apostle Paul concluded the beautiful "love chapter" with these words:

> For we know in part and we prophesy in part, but when perfection comes, the imperfect disappears. When I was a child, . . . I reasoned like a child. When I became a man, I put childish ways behind me. Now we see but a poor reflection [as in a mirror]; *then we shall see face to face*. Now I know in part; then I shall know fully, even as I am fully known (1 Cor. 13:9–12, italics added).

The last chapter of the Bible lists the features of the perfect existence to come after the end of this age.

> On each side of the river stood the tree of life, bearing twelve crops of fruit, yielding its fruit every month. And the leaves of the tree are for the healing of the nations. No longer will there be any curse. The throne of God and of the Lamb will be in the city, and his servants will serve him. *They will see his face,* and his name will be on their foreheads. There will be no more night. They will not need the light of a lamp or the light of the sun, for the Lord God will give them light. And they will reign for ever and ever (Rev. 22:2–5, italics added).

As we look forward, then, to seeing God face to face in an even more beautiful way than Moses did, may we give him all the glory and remember our own smallness. When God calls us into his presence, and when we respond *"Henani"* to that call, let us remember to whisper and take off our shoes.

To God be the glory, great things he hath done,
So loved he the world that he gave us his Son,
Who yielded his life an atonement for sin,
And opened the lifegate that all may go in.

O perfect redemption, the purchase of blood,
To every believer the promise of God;
The vilest offender who truly believes,
That moment from Jesus a pardon receives.

Great things he hath taught us, great things he hath done,
And great our rejoicing through Jesus the Son;
But purer, and higher, and greater will be
Our wonder, our transport, when Jesus we see.

REFRAIN:
Praise the Lord, praise the Lord,
Let the earth hear his voice!
Praise the Lord, praise the Lord,
Let the people rejoice!
O come to the Father through Jesus the Son,
And give him the glory, great things he hath done.

Fanny J. Crosby, 1875

8

Samuel
The Sensitive Self

Primary Scripture Reading

1 Samuel 1–3; 7–13; 15–16; 28

Supplementary Reference

Exodus 29:9
Numbers 18
1 Chronicles 6:26
Hebrews 7–9

Questions for Study and Discussion

1. Why did Hannah name her son Samuel? How was his name an appropriate summary of his long life and relationship with God?

2. How did Samuel recognize and receive God's call? How do you know God's voice and message to you? Who or what helps you to interpret and apply God's Word?

3. To which tribe of Israel did Samuel belong (cf. 1 Sam. 1:1 with 1 Chron. 6:26)? What special office was given by God exclusively to members of that tribe? What rights and responsibilities went with that role? Why was Eli's family cursed by God through an unnamed prophet in 1 Samuel 2:27–36? In what ways was Samuel involved in that prophecy?

4. What did Samuel think about the people's demand for a king? How did his opinion affect his behavior in carrying out his duties?

5. Samuel anointed the first two kings of Israel. How did his relationship and responsibility to each of them differ? Did Samuel act or feel differently toward them? Why or why not?

6. Why did God allow Saul to become Israel's first king, when he knew what would happen? If you know an individual or group of God's people is making some mistake, what can you do about it?

7. In what ways was Samuel's sensitivity to God an asset? How was it also a liability? What risks are you willing to take in asking God to make you more sensitive to his voice?

I know you believe you understand what you thought I said, but I want you to know that what you think you heard is not what I meant!"

This sign, hung in the employee's lounge of a large company, points out in a humorous way a serious problem in communication. Instead of offering the possibility of a bridge of understanding between them, a gulf of isolation is created between speaker and listener, accentuated by the ten personal pronouns, which makes the likelihood of conveying the real message all but hopeless. Each person is focused inwardly on his own processes, rather than being sensitive to the other, in the positive sense of responding readily to outside stimuli.

Samuel helps us to become sensitive selves in our communication with God and his people. From his biblical biography we learn to tune in to the clear message of God, to cut through the static of indifference and disobedience, and to transmit the gospel honestly and joyfully with our words and actions.

Sensitivity Started

The name *Samuel,* which means "heard of God," is both a reflection and a prediction of sensitive communication. When Hannah poured out her heart in prayer before the Lord and promised to dedicate her child to God's service, she *knew* that God had heard and would act perfectly to meet her need. That is why she immediately "went her way and ate something, and her face was no longer downcast" (1 Sam. 1:18), long before "Elkanah lay with Hannah his wife, and the LORD remembered her. . . . Hannah conceived and gave birth to a son. She named him Samuel, saying, 'Because I asked the LORD for him'" (1

Sam. 1:19–21). It would be even more accurate to say that she named the baby Samuel not merely because she had asked the Lord for him but because God had *heard* her prayer.

In contrast, the lack of sensitivity on the part of Eli the priest is already apparent in this passage. When he observed Hannah moving her lips soundlessly, he jumped to the conclusion that she was drunk and rebuked her. She had to explain that what he had assumed to be wickedness was in fact the earnestness of a soul praying out of "anguish and grief" (1 Sam. 1:16). Only then did Eli respond appropriately according to his role: "Go in peace, and may the God of Israel grant you what you have asked of him" (1 Sam. 1:17).

We can only guess how many years elapsed between Hannah's commitment, her conceiving Samuel, and the completion of her vow to give him to the Lord at the tabernacle at Shiloh after he was weaned. Chapter 2 contains her wonderful celebration of God's greatness, and records the fact that she left her little boy with Eli and went home to Ramah with her husband. Then, as though with split-screen cinematography, we follow Hannah home to see God blessing her with many more children; at the same time, we see the contrast between the characters of the men in Samuel's new environment and his own physical and spiritual growth.

"Eli's sons were wicked men" (1 Sam. 2:12). They violated God's principles of worship and sacrifice and abused their priestly privilege by having a portion of each offering reserved for them. They demanded rare steak instead of beef stew. "This sin of the young men was very great in the LORD's sight, for they were treating the LORD's offering with contempt" (1 Sam. 2:17). In addition, there was a scandal involving Hophni and Phineas with the women who served at the entrance to the tabernacle (1 Sam. 2:22). Eli tried to rebuke his sons and recall them to a right relationship of service and purity toward God and all Israel, but they defied his authority (1 Sam. 2:25). Worse, they defiled the tabernacle and corrupted the role of priest in the eyes of the people. God sent an unnamed prophet to inform Eli that because of his sons' sins none of his descendants would live past the prime of life, and that a new priestly line was about to be established:

> Therefore the LORD, the God of Israel, declares, "I promised that your house and your father's house would minister before me forever." But now the LORD declares: "Far be it from me! Those who honor me I will honor, but those who despise me will be disdained. . . . I will raise up for myself a faithful priest, who will do according to what is in my heart and mind. I will firmly establish his house, and he will minister before my anointed one always" (1 Sam 2:30, 35).

This faithful, obedient, sensitive priest was Samuel. Notice that the Levitical priesthood itself was not abolished by this proclamation. Samuel was descended from the Kohathite clan of Levites, though he lived within the territory allotted to Ephraim (cf. 1 Sam. 1:1 with 1 Chron. 6:26). That line of inheritance would continue to be a prerequisite for priests in Israel until Christ appeared to offer a permanent and perfect priesthood, not because of his human ancestry (through the tribe of Judah instead of Levi), but on the basis of better promises and an indestructible life (see Hebrews 7–9).

Simple Sensitivity

The touching story of God's repeated call to little Samuel at midnight is a familiar one. We should realize, however, that it was not so much a dramatic turning point as a significant moment within the ongoing context of God's plan for all his people and his selection and placement of Samuel for service. The verses that describe Samuel's development up to and following that scene show the orientation of his whole life toward God:

> "But Samuel was ministering before the LORD—a boy wearing a linen ephod" (1 Sam. 2:18).
> "Meanwhile, the boy Samuel grew up in the presence of the LORD" (1 Sam. 2:21).
> "And the boy Samuel continued to grow in stature and in favor with the LORD and with men" (1 Sam 2:26).
> "The boy Samuel ministered before the LORD under Eli. In

those days the word of the LORD was rare; there were not many visions" (1 Sam 3:1).

"Then the LORD called Samuel. Samuel answered, 'Here I am [*Henani*].' And he ran to Eli and said, 'Here I am [*Henani*]; you called me'" (1 Sam 3:4).

"Now Samuel did not yet know the LORD: The word of the LORD had not yet been revealed to him" (1 Sam 3:7).

"The LORD came and stood there, calling as at the other times, 'Samuel! Samuel!' Then Samuel said, 'Speak, for your servant is listening'" (1 Sam. 3:10).

"The LORD was with Samuel as he grew up, and he let none of his words fall to the ground. And all Israel from Dan to Beersheba recognized that Samuel was attested as a prophet of the LORD. The LORD continued to appear at Shiloh, and there he revealed himself to Samuel through his word. And Samuel's word came to all Israel" (1 Sam. 3:19—4:1).

Several applications for our own lives may be discovered in the above sequence. First, Samuel was already serving in the tabernacle *before* God's word was fully revealed to him. He did not wait for his "lightning bolt" experience to jolt him to obey what he already knew was God's will. When we dedicate ourselves to God and wait to know in what unique ways he will direct our lives, we don't need to sit idly, either. We can act according to what God clearly wants in every life—to bring glory to his name as we manifest the joy of being his redeemed children.

Second, the circumstances of Samuel's environment did not hinder him from responding to God's call. This principle should encourage us today, as well: where we are physically need not interfere with where we are spiritually. We are wrong to blame our feeble faith on poor role models or a sordid background. It is not the details of our past but the present condition of our hearts that God considers when he calls and empowers us to serve him. This does not mean that there are no consequences to the choices we make concerning our surroundings and companions. But it does offer the hope that external events over which we have no control cannot exclude us from eternal fellowship with God.

Third, God makes person-to-person, not station-to-station

calls. He did not speak with Eli or his evil sons. "In those days the word of the LORD was rare; there were not many visions" (1 Sam. 3:1), we are told. Still, there was one sensitive soul who heard his name called and willingly responded, *"Henani,"* even before he knew enough to recognize God's voice.

Finally, Eli's role should not be left out of the lessons we can learn from this passage. He was nearly blind at this point, but he was not entirely deaf to God's word. Though he was not as sensitive or astute as we might like him to be, or as we might imagine ourselves to be, we must credit Eli with his acceptance and affirmation of God's will when he finally perceived it. He compelled Samuel to tell him everything exactly as God had spoken it, and then said, "He is the LORD; let him do what is good in his eyes" (1 Sam. 3:18).

Thus, God fulfilled his word through the prophet, replacing the self-indulgent priests with the sensitive Samuel, whom he confirmed in the eyes of all the people. Chapters 4–6 then record the Philistines' attack and capture of the ark of God, and finally its return to Israel. Still, twenty years passed before the people were ready to obey God's word and serve him only, as Samuel urged them. Then he interceded for them with confession (1 Sam. 7:5–6) and sacrifice (1 Sam. 7:9–10), leading them to victory and peace (1 Sam. 7:11–14).

During the interlude, Samuel did not stop serving or praying to God:

> Samuel continued as judge over Israel all the days of his life. From year to year he went on a circuit from Bethel to Gilgal to Mizpah, judging Israel in all those places. But he always went back to Ramah, where his home was, and there he also judged Israel. And he built an altar there to the LORD (1 Sam. 7:15–17).

God blessed his ministry as he made the circuit-court rounds in Israel. He also blessed Samuel personally, giving him a home in Ramah, perhaps close to his mother, brothers, and sisters, as well as a wife and children of his own.

As time passed, Samuel appointed his sons to serve as judges with and after him, but they proved no better than Eli's sons had been: "But his sons did not walk in his ways. They turned aside after dishonest gain and accepted bribes and perverted justice" (1 Sam. 8:3). Here we have the counterpart to our earlier principle: A godly role model or environment does *not* guarantee a good relationship with God, any more than a poor background precludes it. The quality of our heart's response is evaluated on an individual basis—there are no piggyback rides either to eternal separation or to blessing.

Solo Sensitivity

So far, we have seen the establishment of Samuel as priest, prophet, and judge in Israel at a crucial moment in its history. He heard and responded faithfully to God's call in a time when even the priests were dull of sense and heart. As we go on with his story, we discover some of the risks of such sensitivity: it can be lonely and painful to be the only one attuned to God's voice when the people turn away from him. The first hint of tension appears in chapter 8:

> So all the elders of Israel gathered together and came to Samuel at Ramah. They said to him, "You are old, and your sons do not walk in your ways; now appoint a king to lead us, such as all the other nations have."
> But when they said, "Give us a king to lead us," this displeased Samuel; so he prayed to the LORD (1 Sam. 8:4–6).

The church has drawn many lessons from the conformist attitude inherent in the people's demand for a king, which don't need to be repeated here. A less common but equally important point comes out of Samuel's feelings and actions in response to their words: "This displeased Samuel; so he prayed to the LORD." Both phrases are significant. Samuel did not shrug off his displeasure, pretend to be cheerful or indifferent, or attempt to talk himself out of his honest reaction. He truly grieved over the people's demands, because his heart was bound up in God's heart; the rejection of his leadership was identical with rejection of God's leadership, and the implications were devastating. Samuel neither swallowed nor wallowed in his personal perspective;

he recognized his reaction, "so he prayed to the LORD." He didn't say to himself, "Oh, I really shouldn't feel this way," or "I'm sure it won't do God any good to hear this." His sensitivity is evident in this passage both in his own sense of outrage and in his faithful function as a precise transmitter of messages between God and Israel. Notice the following verses: "Samuel told all the words of the LORD to the people who were asking him for a king" (1 Sam. 8:10); "When Samuel heard all that the people said, he repeated it before the LORD. . . . Then Samuel said to the men of Israel, 'Everyone go back to his own town'" (1 Sam. 8:21–22).

God told Samuel to warn the people of the consequences of having a king. He also confirmed Samuel in his role and comforted him with assurances of His sovereignty and love:

> "Listen to all that the people are saying to you; it is not you they have rejected as their king, but me. As they have done from the day I brought them up out of Egypt until this day, forsaking me and serving other gods, so they are doing to you. Now listen to them; but warn them solemnly and let them know what the king who will reign over them will do" (1 Sam. 8:7–9).

Once Saul became king, Samuel continued to fulfill his role of representing God's Word and will to the people; he continued to intercede on their behalf, as well. This task meant he left himself open to the pain of rejection and misunderstanding, to seeing the nation turn away from his call to obedience and blessing in spite of his repeated good counsel and example. Several times he reminded them of their history and of the consistent character of God:

> "Do not be afraid. . . . You have done all this evil; yet do not turn away from the LORD, but serve the LORD with all your heart. Do not turn away after useless idols. They can do you no good, nor can they rescue you, because they are useless. For the sake of his great name the LORD will not reject his people, because the LORD was pleased to make you his own. As for me, far be it from me that I should sin against the LORD by failing to pray for you. And I will teach you the way that is good and right. But be sure to fear the

LORD and serve him faithfully with all your heart; consider what great things he has done for you. Yet if you persist in doing evil, both you and your king will be swept away" (1 Sam. 12:20–25).

Samuel also tried to communicate God's plans to King Saul directly, but with little effect. They simply were not on the same wavelength. After Samuel anointed Saul, he gave him a series of signs, all of which were confirmed, and then instructed him to wait seven days until he arrived to make the appropriate sacrifices (1 Sam. 10:7–9). But the Philistines prepared to attack, and the Israelites who were gathered to Saul were "quaking with fear" (1 Sam. 13:7). Impatient Saul took matters into his own hands and offered the sacrifices himself, an act which demonstrated his own lack of sensitivity to God's designs both for proper leadership and for worship. Samuel rebuked him:

> You acted foolishly. . . . You have not kept the command the LORD your God gave you; if you had, he would have established your kingdom over Israel for all time. But now your kingdom will not endure; the LORD has sought out a man after his own heart and appointed him leader of his people, because you have not kept the LORD's command (1 Sam. 13:13–14).

Still, God gave Saul another chance to prove himself:

> Samuel said to Saul, "I am the one the LORD sent to anoint you the king over his people Israel; so listen now to the message from the LORD. This is what the LORD Almighty says: 'I will punish the Amalekites for what they did to Israel when they waylaid them as they came up from Egypt. Now go, attack the Amalekites and totally destroy everything that belongs to them. Do not spare them; put to death men and women, children and infants, cattle and sheep, camels and donkeys" (1 Sam. 15:1–3).

Notice that Samuel was careful to identify himself as "the one the LORD sent," and that he was faithful to deliver God's message verbatim. Samuel had his own opinion about Saul, no doubt, and knew the uselessness of trying to penetrate his stubborn, selfish spirit; but he remained true to his own calling as prophet and judge. The continuing closeness between Samuel and God contrasts sharply with the increasing distance between the LORD and the king of his people, as Saul once again disobeyed his clear command.

> Then the word of the LORD came to Samuel: "I am grieved that I have made Saul king, because he has turned away from me and has not carried out my instructions." Samuel was troubled, and he cried out to the LORD all that night.
>
> Early in the morning Samuel got up and went to meet Saul, but he was told, "Saul has gone to Carmel. There he has set up a monument in his own honor and has turned and gone on down to Gilgal."
>
> When Samuel reached him, Saul said, "The LORD bless you! I have carried out the LORD's instructions."
>
> But Samuel said, "What then is this bleating of sheep in my ears? What is this lowing of cattle that I hear?"
>
> Saul answered, "The soldiers brought them from the Amalekites; they spared the best of the sheep and cattle to sacrifice to the LORD your God, but we totally destroyed the rest."
>
> "Stop!" Samuel said to Saul. "Let me tell you what the LORD said to me last night."
>
> "Tell me," Saul replied.
>
> Samuel said, "Although you were once small in your own eyes, did you not become the head of the tribes of Israel? The LORD anointed you king over Israel. And he sent you on a mission, saying, 'Go, and completely destroy those wicked people, the Amalekites; make war on them until you have wiped them out.' Why did you not obey the LORD? Why did you pounce on the plunder and do evil in the eyes of the LORD?" (1 Sam. 15:10–20).

Saul made a feeble effort to defend himself, but Samuel continued,

> "Does the LORD delight in burnt
>   offerings and sacrifices
> as much as in obeying the voice of the LORD?
> To obey is better than sacrifice,
>   and to heed is better than the fat of rams.
> For rebellion is like the sin of divination,
>   and arrogance like the evil of idolatry.

> Because you have rejected the word of the LORD,
> he has rejected you as king" (1 Sam. 15:22–23).

Samuel's message straight from God had fallen on deaf ears once again. Chapter 15 ends sadly: "Then Samuel left for Ramah, but Saul went up to his home in Gibeah of Saul. Until the day Samuel died, he did not go to see Saul again, though Samuel mourned for him. And the LORD was grieved that he had made Saul king over Israel." Again we see the parallel emotions of Samuel and his God.

Satisfied Sensitivity

Their sadness did not last long. "The LORD said to Samuel, 'How long will you mourn for Saul, since I have rejected him as king over Israel? Fill your horn with oil and be on your way; I am sending you to Jesse of Bethlehem. I have chosen one of his sons to be king'" (1 Sam. 16:1). God got Samuel on his feet once again for service. Verse 4 is a succinct summary of the whole of his life: "Samuel did what the LORD said." He heard and heeded, as always, following God's clear commands even when he did not fully understand them. So David was selected and anointed as the next king of Israel, not because he looked the part, but rather because he was right in his heart toward God.

Samuel then faded from prominence, as David entered into close communion with his Lord, "and from that day on the Spirit of the LORD came upon David in power. Samuel then went to Ramah" (1 Sam. 16:13). David went to him once, after escaping Saul's attempt to kill him (1 Sam. 19:18–24), but the fact of Samuel's death is not mentioned until after Saul went to the extreme measure of going to a medium to call him up: "Now Samuel was dead, and all Israel had mourned for him and buried him in his own town of Ramah" (1 Sam. 28:3). In that bizarre episode, the spirit of Samuel offered Saul nothing but a recorded message of what God had said, and Saul had ignored, previously.

Meanwhile, we see Samuel's spirit of sensitivity carried on in the future king: "But David found strength in the LORD his God."

Samuel's function had been fulfilled. His lonely vigil keeping his ear on God's heartbeat was ended. Although he and David did not enjoy a long period of fellowship as two kindred souls in the service of the Lord, Samuel must have experienced deep satisfaction as he recognized God's good hands powerfully at work on behalf of his people and in spite of their continued rebellion, placing his kingdom in devoted, if still human, hands.

Samuel was never a hero in the sense of performing "above and beyond the call of duty." Only in passing is he mentioned on the roll call of the faithful in Hebrews 11. But he is worthy of our appreciation and our imitation if we desire to develop our own sensitivity toward God. Before we respond *"Henani"* and pray to become more spiritually tuned in to God's heart as Samuel and David were, we should consider that the periods of isolation, rejection, and grief Samuel experienced are likely consequences of such heightened awareness. If we allow the protective shells in which we hide to be cracked open, if we become more vulnerable to express God's plan and power more visibly, we will undoubtedly feel real pain. But we can also know the joy of sharing in the suffering of Christ to share in his glory (Phil. 3:10).

> Speak, Lord, in the stillness while I wait on thee;
> Hushed my heart to listen in expectancy.
>
> Speak, O blessed master in this quiet hour;
> Let me see thy face, Lord, feel thy touch of power.
>
> For the words thou speakest, they are life indeed;
> Living bread from heaven, now my spirit feed!
>
> All to thee is yielded, I am not my own;
> Blissful, glad surrender, I am thine alone.
>
> Fill me with the knowledge of thy glorious will;
> All thine own good pleasure in thy child fulfill.
>
> E. May Grimes, 1920

9

David
The Submissive Self

Primary Scripture Readings

2 Samuel 15–16
Psalm 18, 27, 51

Supplementary References

Exodus 25:15
Leviticus 10:1–3
Numbers 4:5–6, 15
Deuteronomy 10:8
1 Samuel 6, 17–21, 24–25, 30
2 Samuel 1–2, 5–7, 11–12, 15, 18
1 Kings 1–2
1 Chronicles 16
Hebrews 9

Questions for Study and Discussion

1. Scan the chapters in 1 and 2 Samuel, listed above, for a quick overview of David's life. Notice David's relationships with the various members of his family, with his nation, and with God.

2. Identify several key events which you consider either high or low moments for David. Try to express the essence of David's personality and motivation by completing the following sentences with specific examples: "David was more than anything else a man of _____. His conduct in dealing with _____, _____, and _____ suggests that _____ was more important to David than anything or anyone else."

3. Read the references to the ark in Exodus, Leviticus, Numbers, and Deuteronomy, and the explanation of its symbolism and purpose for the Christian in Hebrews 9. Describe the ark and its function. How was it regarded by Saul, by the Philistines, and by David?

4. What did David learn from his series of experiences connected with the ark? Do you find a change in David's attitude toward God as a result? Ultimately, what did David want to do for God? What did he get to do?

5. In what ways is David a very significant figure in the New Testament? Find and share verses that demonstrate his importance. Why should he be important to the Christian today?

6. Enjoy the rich heritage of David's psalms, written in different periods of his life. Include Psalm 3, 18, 22, 27, 34, 51, and any others that you find meaningful. What insights into the character of David do they give you? List verses you find beautiful and revealing. How do David's feelings expressed in the Psalms help you to respond more willingly to God's call to you?

Be ye doers of the word, and not hearers only, deceiving your own selves," Jesus' brother James admonished believers (James 1:22 KJV). But our willingness to hear and to do God's will doesn't always mean we should take prompt action. Sometimes God calls to us to tell us no, or to stop us from proceeding down a wrong path on our own initiative. Most of us have experienced the truth of Romans 7:15: "I do not understand what I do. For what I want to do I do not do, but what I hate I do." It is often as hard *not* to do what we want to do but shouldn't, as it is to do something we may not feel like doing.

King David was an expert at waiting for and following God's lead, at least most of the time. "Wait on the LORD: be of good courage, and he shall strengthen thine heart: wait, I say, on the LORD" was a common theme in his psalms (Ps. 27:14 KJV). When he obeyed his own advice, David was blessed; when he went ahead, against, or around God's directions, trouble followed. But David always came back to God, accepting first his chastisement and then his forgiveness. This man of strength learned many painful lessons in true submission that we can apply to the situations when God must intervene in our lives to keep us from taking a wrong path.

Before beginning our consideration of David (what study of Old Testament men could leave him out?) I must confess that he does not exactly qualify as one who said *Henani* to God, at least not in Scripture's original manuscripts, that we know.

The term translated "Here am I" in 2 Samuel 15:26 comes from the Hebrew זֶּה , pronounced "zeh," which is simply a demonstrative pronoun indicating *this* one, *this* time, *this* place. Nevertheless, it is not inappropriate to include David on our roster for this course of study. Even though not in so many words, David expressed his reverent yielding to God, a trait we can follow through four areas of his life as a whole: his family, friends and followers, failings, and faith in the future.

Family

A man I know had four daughters. The family joke was that when he introduced them to guests, he added taglines to each of their names: "This one is the smartest, this the prettiest, this the nicest, and that's the youngest." A funny line for all but one, the poor youngest! The scene in 1 Samuel 16 is similar. God told Samuel to go to Jesse and anoint one of his sons to be king in place of the rejected Saul, who had looked the part but had not honored God with his whole heart (1 Sam. 13:13–14; 15:17–28). Samuel thought Eliab, the eldest son, would fit the crown just fine, but the Lord reminded him, "Do not consider his appearance or his height, for I have rejected him. The LORD does not look at the things man looks at. Man looks at the outward appearance, but the LORD looks at the heart" (1 Sam. 16:7). One by one the seven sons of Jesse were brought before Samuel, who listened carefully for God's signal each time and finally said, "The LORD has not chosen these. Are these all the sons you have?" Jesse then admitted there was one more. "There is still the youngest, but he is tending the sheep." The attitude peeked through Jesse's words, I think, that David didn't count for much.

He was an afterthought, reliably doing his duty in the hills or running errands for the others, but not a full participant in the daily routines of the household, and certainly not a likely candidate for king. What a surprise it must have been for Jesse to hear that Samuel would not proceed with the sacrifice without David, and then to see David anointed in the presence of his brothers at God's command!

It is interesting to note that other people seemed to think more highly of David, and more often, than did his own family. When he was finally brought to Samuel, he made a fine impression. "He was ruddy, with a fine appearance, and handsome features" (1 Sam. 16:12). The Spirit of the Lord came upon David in power after his anointing, but it departed from King Saul. When the king ordered his attendants to find someone to cheer him with music, one of the servants answered promptly, "I have seen a son of Jesse of Bethlehem who knows how to play the harp. He is a brave man and a warrior. He speaks well and is a fine-looking man. And the Lord is with him" (1 Sam. 16:18). Do you suppose David's own father would have given him such a high recommendation?

When Jesse sent David to Saul, he added a donkey loaded with bread, a skin of wine, and a young goat to the package. These fine gifts were expressive of Jesse's love and loyalty to his king, but they also may have reflected a father's concern to make David more acceptable. Perhaps Jesse was again somewhat surprised by Saul's reaction: "Allow David to remain in my service, for I am pleased with him" (1 Sam. 16:22).

David's victory over Goliath in the name of the Lord Almighty was a wonderful testimony to his faith. It is also an opportunity for us to observe his brothers' opinion of him. When he first arrived at the camp, he deposited the ten loaves and cheeses with the keeper of supplies and ran to greet his brothers. When he saw Goliath and sensed the fear in the hearts of the Israelites, he wanted to know more.

> When Eliab, David's oldest brother, heard him speaking with the men, he burned with anger at him and asked, "Why have you come down here? And with whom did you leave those few sheep in the desert? I know how conceited you are and how wicked your heart is; you came down only to watch the battle."
>
> "Now what have I done?" said David. "Can't I even speak?" (1 Sam. 17:28–29).

Obviously, David's brother was not very happy to see him, and tried to use the occasion to put him down. Even after David killed the giant, his brothers didn't seem to take part in his triumph, and they are not mentioned again for five more chapters.

Instead, David found love and support in his friendship with Jonathan. When he first fled from Saul, he was alone. He attracted a band of malcontents, including his family, some time later.

> David left Gath and escaped to the cave of Adullam. When his brothers and his father's household heard about it, they went down to him there. All those who were in distress or in debt or discontented gathered around him, and he became their leader. About four hundred men were with him (1 Sam. 22:1–2).

David did not seem to harbor resentment against his family for the numerous times they slighted him. Instead, he focused on the power of God and trusted in his promises. Aside from his dealings with his father and older brothers, David also suffered mistreatment by his cousin Joab and several of his own sons who rebelled against him. But rather than claiming innocence or blaming others for his trials, he bore the responsibility for the effects of his sins on his family.

It was in the context of Absalom's rebellion that David uttered these words, here quoted from the King James Version:

> And all the country wept with a loud voice, and all the people passed over: the king also himself passed over the brook Kidron, and all the people passed over, toward the way of the wilderness.

And lo Zadok also, and all the Levites *were* with him, bearing the ark of the covenant of God: and they set down the ark of God; and Abiathar went up, until all the people had done passing out of the city.

And the king said unto Zadok, Carry back the ark of God into the city: if I shall find favor in the eyes of the LORD, he will bring me again, and shew me *both* it, and his habitation;

But if he thus say, I have no delight in thee; behold, *here am I*, let him do to me as seemeth good unto him (2 Sam. 15:23–26, italics added in v. 26).

David's submissive tone was not an admission of weakness in the face of his son's opposition, but rather an affirmation of strong faith in his Lord. He was showing reverence for the ark, and an understanding of the fact that it was in God alone and not in any magic inherent in the holy box that real protection resided. More specifically, he was demonstrating that he had learned the lesson of 2 Samuel 6, when God had killed a man for irreverently touching the ark:

When they came to the threshing floor of Nacon, Uzzah reached out and took hold of the ark of God, because the oxen stumbled. The LORD's anger burned against Uzzah because of his irreverent act; therefore God struck him down and he died there beside the ark of God.

Then David was angry because the LORD's wrath had broken out against Uzzah, and to this day that place is called Perez Uzzah.

David was afraid of the LORD that day and said, "How can the ark of the LORD ever come to me?" He was not willing to take the ark of the LORD to be with him in the City of David. Instead, he took it aside to the house of Obed-Edom the Gittite. The ark of the LORD remained in the house of Obed-Edom the Gittite for three months, and the LORD blessed him and his entire household.

Now King David was told, "The LORD has blessed the household of Obed-Edom and everything he has, because of the ark of God." So David went down and brought up the ark of God from the house of Obed-Edom to the City of David with rejoicing.

> When those who were carrying the ark of the LORD had taken six
> steps, he sacrificed a bull and a fattened calf. David, wearing a
> linen ephod, danced before the LORD with all his might, while
> he and the entire house of Israel brought up the ark of the LORD
> with shouts and the sound of trumpets (2 Sam. 6:6–15).

David's anger and fear toward God were transformed into great
rejoicing when the ark had been carried into Jerusalem at that
time; in this instance he showed he was unwilling to move it
again, but his attitude was one of calm confidence, awe, and
devotion.

David did not seek revenge against those who defied him for
personal reasons. Perhaps it was Abigail who helped him to
maintain a proper sense of God's perspective and priorities in
the face of insults (see 1 Sam. 25). Yet, David did distinguish
between threats to himself, which were brought on by his own
actions and which had to be endured during his lifetime, and
threats to the strength and security of the kingdom, which could
not be tolerated after his death. Although he had done nothing
to quell Shimei's curses or Joab's mutiny while he was king,
David charged Solomon to have both of these men killed, in
order that the kingdom be "firmly established" (1 Kings 2).

Friends and Followers

David's submissive spirit may also be seen in his relationships
with his friends and followers. His closest friend was Jonathan,
Saul's son.

> After David had finished talking with Saul, Jonathan became
> one in spirit with David, and he loved him as himself. From that
> day Saul kept David with him and did not let him return to his
> father's house. And Jonathan made a covenant with David be-
> cause he loved him as himself. Jonathan took off the robe he was
> wearing and gave it to David, along with his tunic, and even his
> sword, his bow and his belt (1 Sam. 18:1–4).

David had refused Saul's armor when he battled Goliath, because it did not fit and he was not used to it. But he accepted

Jonathan's clothing and weapons, because they were gifts of true devotion. Several times Jonathan proved his love by risking his own safety to warn David of Saul's intentions to kill him (1 Sam. 19:1–7; 20:1–42). When they parted for the last time,

> they kissed each other and wept together—but David wept the most.
>
> Jonathan said to David, "Go in peace, for we have sworn friendship with each other in the name of the LORD, saying, 'The LORD is witness between you and me, and between your descendants and my descendants forever.'" Then David left, and Jonathan went back to the town (1 Sam. 20:41–42).

David and Jonathan were bound together by a covenant of love that stretched across even the mountain of Saul's mania. After the death of Jonathan and Saul, David kept his promise not to harm Jonathan's descendants by bringing his lame son, Mephibosheth, to his table, a clear demonstration of his provision and protection (2 Sam. 9). Though deceived for a time by Ziba, Mephibosheth's steward, who claimed that his master was plotting to regain the throne of his grandfather Saul (2 Sam. 16), David later made restitution (2 Sam. 19:24–30).

David's concern for his followers, and their love for him, are again evident in 2 Samuel 23:

> During harvest time, three of the thirty chief men came down to David at the cave of Adullam, while a band of Philistines was encamped in the Valley of Rephaim. At that time David was in the stronghold, and the Philistine garrison was at Bethlehem. David longed for water and said, "Oh, that someone would get me a drink of water from the well near the gate of Bethlehem!" So the three mighty men broke through the Philistine lines, drew water from the well near the gate of Bethlehem and carried it back to David. But he refused to drink it; instead, he poured it out before the LORD. "Far be it from me, O LORD, to do this!" he said. "Is it not the blood of men who went at the risk of their lives?" And David would not drink it (2 Sam. 23:13–17).

Haven't you wondered at the reactions of the "three mighty men" who risked their lives to bring their king exactly what he asked for—not just a drink of water but water from a particular well that happened to lie behind enemy lines—only to have him pour it on the ground when they gave it to him? At first they must have been puzzled, perhaps even irritated, at his lack of appreciation. Not that they necessarily expected thank-you notes, or even military promotions; he was the king, after all, and they were bound to serve him. But he could at least have drunk the water they went to such trouble to get! Wasn't he being rather capricious?

No. David was in fact deeply moved by the devotion his men expressed in this dangerous act. But he would not accept such love for himself alone, when it was God who had placed him as leader over such people. The water became a true libation, a drink offering, in praise of the almighty God. Rather than treating their gift lightly, he gave it greater significance by humbly sacrificing it to the Lord.

I once attended a recital by the great soprano Leontyne Price. A packed Carnegie Hall audience raved and cheered, screamed, and threw flowers. After every encore, the prima donna bowed and smiled graciously, accepting more and more roses as admirers rushed to the stage. Finally, she closed her eyes and pointed heavenward—an unashamed gesture of praise to her Lord, who had given her a beautiful voice. The flowers were not cast aside, but offered up, elevated to an expression of true worship. When you receive tokens of affection or admiration, do you point the bouquets heavenward in thanksgiving to the one from whom all blessings flow?

Failings

David exemplified the best human qualities of leadership and service, strength and humility, but he was still human. He was a man after God's own heart, but he was not perfect. He did not always submit his plans to God before pursuing them.

When he fled from Saul, David acted on his own initiative to get food and weapons from the priests at Nob. Then he went to Achish, king of Gath, enemy of Israel, where he had to feign madness to protect himself when he was identified. When Doeg reported to Saul that the priests of Nob had helped David, Saul had eighty-five priests and the whole town slaughtered. David grieved when he learned the consequences of his actions, but he did not excuse them.

> But Abiathar, a son of Ahimelech son of Ahitub, escaped and fled to join David. He told David that Saul had killed the priests of the LORD. Then David said to Abiathar: "That day, when Doeg the Edomite was there, I knew he would be sure to tell Saul. I am responsible for the death of your father's whole family. Stay with me; don't be afraid; the man who is seeking your life is seeking mine also. You will be safe with me" (1 Sam. 22:20–23).

David had failed, but in dealing with his failures he acted honorably.

An even more memorable failure is recorded in 2 Samuel 11, when David again acted independently to obtain something he wanted. Only at the end of the long string of events regarding his affair with Bathsheba and the murder of her husband do we read the final phrase: "But the thing David had done displeased the LORD" (2 Sam. 11:27). Obviously, pleasing God had not been uppermost in David's mind during the stages of actual intrigue. Yet when God sent Nathan the prophet to confront David with his sin, his true colors were revealed once again.

> Then Nathan said to David, "You are the man! . . .
> Then David said to Nathan, "I have sinned against the LORD."
> Nathan replied, "The LORD has taken away your sin. You are not going to die. But because by doing this you have made the enemies of the LORD show utter contempt, the son born to you will die." . . .
> On the seventh day the child died. David's servants were afraid to tell him that the child was dead, for they thought, "While the child was still living, we spoke to David but he would not listen to us. How can we tell him the child is dead? He may do something desperate." . . .
> Then David got up from the ground. After he had washed, put on lotions and changed his clothes, he went into the house

of the LORD and worshiped. Then he went to his own house, and at his request they served him food, and he ate. . . . He answered, "While the child was still alive, I fasted and wept. I thought, 'Who knows? The LORD may be gracious to me and let the child live.' But now that he is dead, why should I fast? Can I bring him back again? I will go to him, but he will not return to me."

Then David comforted his wife Bathsheba, and he went to her and lay with her. She gave birth to a son, and they named him Solomon. The LORD loved him; and because the LORD loved him, he sent word through Nathan the prophet to name him Jedidiah" (2 Sam. 12:1–25 *passim*).

David's submissive spirit toward God in acknowledging his sin forthrightly, without any excuses, is challenging to us in our age of rampant self-justification. David also accepted God's judgment in taking the child's life, though he prayed that it might be spared. His behavior after learning that the child was dead surprised his servants, but was consistent with his submissive heart. Then he comforted his wife. God's love, expressed in the sending of a special name for Solomon, also showed his pleasure in David's attitude throughout this sequence. The birth of the next king proved that God had indeed taken away David's sin, as he had promised.

Have you puzzled over the fact that God's best man could commit such crimes and still be forgiven, even remain a favorite? Aren't you comforted by the fact that he did? It is important to realize that David's failings, his series of sins in regard to Bathsheba and many others, did not bring to an end his close relationship with his holy God. His response to the confrontation, the judgment, and the restoration marked a new level of true obedience and even greater faith. God holds up a high standard of moral conduct for his people, but he does not cease to manifest his love when we fall, if we will humbly accept his correction. Will you put off inappropriate mourning over your past sins, and choose instead to get up, get washed, get dressed, and get on with the joy of worship, as David did? Then you can expect to see new birth in your life as well.

Faith in the Future

David submitted to his sovereign Lord's plans for the future for himself, his family, and his nation. He refused to "touch the LORD's anointed," as he repeatedly called King Saul, although he had at least two apparently perfect opportunities to seize the promised kingdom prematurely (see 1 Sam. 24 and 26). Even as he cut Saul's robe and took the water jug and spear from near Saul's head, David knew that God would give him the kingdom in due time, without his needing to take Saul's life. With these tokens, he demanded that Saul, and even his own men, acknowledge his restraint and his good intentions toward the king, a further testimony to his faith.

Do you have the same confidence David showed in waiting for God's promises? In Luke 12, Jesus comforted his disciples with assurances of God's care for his own:

> Therefore I tell you, do not worry about your life, what you will eat; or about your body, what you will wear. Life is more than food, and the body more than clothes. Consider the ravens: They do not sow or reap, they have no storeroom or barn; yet God feeds them. And how much more valuable you are than birds! Who of you by worrying can add a single hour to his life? Since you cannot do this very little thing, why do you worry about the rest?
>
> Consider how the lilies grow. They do not labor or spin. Yet I tell you, not even Solomon in all his splendor was dressed like one of these. If that is how God clothes the grass of the field, which is here today, and tomorrow is thrown into the fire, how much more will he clothe you, O you of little faith! And do not set your heart on what you will eat or drink; do not worry about it. For the pagan world runs after all such things, and your Father knows that you need them. But seek his kingdom, and these things will be given to you as well.
>
> Do not be afraid, little flock, for your Father has been pleased to give you the kingdom (Luke 12:22–32).

David the shepherd trusted his Father to care for him as a sheep, providing everything he needed at just the right time (Ps. 23).

Do you worry about, or look forward to, the future, when your shepherd, Jesus, has promised to give you an even greater kingdom?

Throughout his life, David's chief end was to glorify his great God. When he was fully established on the throne of Israel and there was peace in the land, he confided to Nathan the prophet, "Here I am, living in a palace of cedar, while the ark of God remains in a tent" (2 Sam. 7:2). Without first consulting God for directions, Nathan readily endorsed the king's plans: "Whatever you have in mind, go ahead and do it, for the LORD is with you" (v. 3).

That night, God told Nathan to stop David from building a temple. It was not David's task to perform—he was a man of blood. But his son Solomon would carry out the project, and David could help to get everything ready. God also gave clear promises that he would establish David's house "forever," a word repeated three times in 2 Samuel 7:5–16.

Of course, David was deeply moved by God's response, and worship poured from his soul:

> Who am I, O Sovereign LORD, and what is my family, that you have brought me this far? And as if this were not enough in your sight, O Sovereign LORD, you have also spoken about the future of the house of your servant. Is this your usual way of dealing with man, O Sovereign LORD?
>
> What more can David say to you? For you know your servant, O Sovereign LORD. For the sake of your word and according to your will, you have done this great thing and made it known to your servant.
>
> How great you are, O Sovereign LORD! There is no one like you, and there is no God but you. . . .
>
> And now, LORD God, keep forever the promise you have made concerning your servant and his house. Do as you promised, so that your name will be great forever. Then men will say, "The LORD Almighty is God over Israel!" And the house of your servant David will be established before you.
>
> O LORD Almighty, God of Israel, you have revealed this to

your servant, saying "I will build a house for you." So your servant has found courage to offer you this prayer. O Sovereign LORD, you are God! Your words are trustworthy, and you have promised these good things to your servant. Now be pleased to bless the house of your servant, that it may continue forever in your sight; for you, O Sovereign LORD, have spoken, and with your blessing the house of your servant will be blessed forever (2 Sam. 7:18–22, 25–29).

Notice how David used God's own words to praise him and claim his promises. We have God's promises preserved in the Scriptures so that we, too, can use them to praise him and count on his continual care. Just as we can trace God's faithfulness in preserving David's line throughout Israel's history and in bringing his own Son to earth as part of this family, we can trust God with our own lives and with the future of our families.

Submission is a negatively loaded word in our culture today. A submissive man is considered a weakling, a wimp, without courage or strength. Even women of strong faith struggle over the application of Paul's instructions to submit to their husbands (Eph. 5:22, Col. 3:18), because it sometimes seems to connote a degradation, a loss of self. But God has always connected submission to obedience, faith, and right relationships. What David knew and exemplified was that true submission to God was possible, appropriate, and required, and that it could be expressed in all the ways he went about his business in the world as well. The joyful yielding to God that we have been tracing through the *Henani* passages of these Old Testament men is visible in the warp and woof of David's life. Is the same principle evident in the way you live, whether you say the word or not?

Great is thy faithfulness, O God my Father,
There is no shadow of turning with thee;
Thou changest not, thy compassions they fail not;
As thou hast been thou forever wilt be.

Summer and winter, and springtime and harvest,
Sun, moon, and stars in their courses above

Join with all nature in manifold witness
To thy great faithfulness, mercy and love.

Pardon for sin and a peace that endureth,
Thy own dear presence to cheer and to guide;
Strength for today and bright hope for tomorrow,
Blessings all mine, with ten thousand beside!

REFRAIN:
Great is thy faithfulness!
Great is thy faithfulness!
Morning by morning new mercies I see;
All I have needed thy hand hath provided—
Great is thy faithfulness,
Lord, unto me!

Thomas O. Chisholm, 1923

10

Isaiah
The Self Sealed by the Spirit

Primary Scripture Readings

2 Chronicles 26:22
Isaiah 6

Supplementary References

Genesis 19:24–29
Exodus 13:21; 31:13; 33:20
Leviticus 11:44; 19:2; 20:7–8, 26
Numbers 19
1 Kings 18:38–39
Psalm 53
Isaiah 1, 7, 9, 11, 12, 43, 54, 55, 65
Zechariah 13:9
Matthew 28:18–20
John 10
Acts 10; 11:9
Romans 7; 12:1
Ephesians 1:13–14; 4; 5:2
Hebrews 9; 12:14, 29; 13:10
1 Peter 1:15–16
Revelation 5

Questions for Study and Discussion

1. Under which kings of Judah did Isaiah serve as prophet? Were they good or bad kings? What effects did Isaiah's messages have on the nation, do you think? Find several examples of events predicted by Isaiah which have been fulfilled. Which of his prophecies speak of times still in the future?

2. From whom did Isaiah get his authority as a prophet? What do you learn about the character of God from his words? Cite specific passages you find especially meaningful.

3. Rephrase Isaiah 6 in your own words, trying to capture the main actions and emotions. Who did what, and how did they feel about it? As an extra challenge, try to express these ideas as a piece of poetry or a miniplay.

4. Why did Isaiah feel "ruined" (NIV), "undone" (KJV), and "unclean" in God's presence? What happened to turn his attitude completely around? How can you overcome your feelings of unworthiness to face God?

5. The holiness of God is stressed in Isaiah 6. Use the references listed above, and other passages you may know, to find places where God speaks of his own holiness and his requirement of holiness in his people. How can this condition be met, do you think? How holy does God consider you to be?

6. Do you find any evidence of the Holy Spirit at work in Isaiah's life, at the beginning or throughout the course of his ministry as a prophet? How was he sealed for service? How can you find the same strength and security for your life?

M y lips are sealed," my father used to tease when he refused to let me wheedle any secret information out of him. His words always brought to mind a plastic bag with its edges permanently interlocked to preserve freshness and prevent leakage. No chance of any stray tidbit slipping out. He was absolutely sealed for silence.

When the Angel of the Lord sealed Isaiah's lips with a burning coal from the altar fire, it was not with the intent of shutting him up. On the contrary, it was to cleanse and commission him for service as a great prophet, and to give him courage to endure rejection when his warnings from God were repeatedly ignored by the people and then ultimately fulfilled by God. When Isaiah immediately responded, *"Henani,"* it was with complete awareness of his own inadequacy and of God's enabling sufficiency.

The Book of Isaiah is the longest and perhaps one of the most difficult to comprehend. It seems to go on and on rather redundantly in negative terms about God using one nation to punish another. But it is also one of the most beautiful and comforting books in the entire Bible. We find here many promises of the coming Christ (Isa. 7, 9), pictures of prosperity and peace at the end of the latter days (chapters 11, 65), and in between, assurances of God's constant presence in our present trials:

> But now, this is what the LORD says—he who created you, O Jacob,
> he who formed you, O Israel;
> "Fear not, for I have redeemed you;
> I have summoned you by name; you are mine.
> When you pass through the waters, I will be with you;
> and when you pass through the rivers, they will not sweep over you.
> When you walk through the fire, you will not be burned;
> the flames will not set you ablaze.
> For I am the LORD, your God, the Holy One of Israel, your Savior (Isa. 43:1–3).

No wonder so many of its passages have been gloriously set to music! Even if you have shied away from it in the past, let me invite you now to read through the book at one sitting, to savor its majestic beauty and to ponder the significance of its revelation for its own time and for ours. Delving into the full mystery is beyond our purpose here, but two general comments will help to place the sixth chapter, which is our focus, in its context within the book as a whole.

First, Isaiah's name means "The Lord saves," a phrase that comprises an apt summary of Isaiah's whole theme. Other nations cannot save, idols cannot save, we cannot save ourselves. Only the Lord, "The Holy One of Israel," saves, and he shall indeed. Although the Lord is also portrayed as the only one who avenges dishonor to his name and carries out judgment against the rebelliousness of his people, there is yet great love in his anger, for he woos his children back to obedience that he might keep his promises of eternal blessing.

Second, I believe that Isaiah was a real person, a single human individual standing in history. In addition to writing this book of prophecy, we are told that Isaiah also kept a chronicle of the life of King Uzziah, who reigned in Judah from 792 to 740 B.C. (2 Chron. 26:22). Scholars calculate that Isaiah may have lived until as late as 681 B.C., when, Jewish tradition suggests, he was sawed in half (see introductory notes to Isaiah and also note on Heb. 11:37 in *NIV Study Bible*). A difficulty arises, then, when we find Isaiah naming King Cyrus of Persia (Isa. 44:28; 45:13), who did not come to power until 539 B.C., as the agent through whom the Israelites would be permitted to return from captivity to their own land. Some critics conclude that the original Isaiah could not have known such a detail, and so posit multiple Isaiahs or an anonymous editor who later amended the text to match subsequent events.

How you feel about these questions of authorship and prophetic authority will affect the extent to which you take seriously and apply personally the lessons of Isaiah 6, to which we now turn our attention. As we consider Isaiah's selection and consecration, we need also to examine our own shortcomings and God's solution when he calls us to his service.

Authority

Isaiah was a prophet, one called to speak forth the words of God. The words he spoke were at times comforting, but most often condemning, even shocking in their vivid portrayal of Israel's impending doom. Furthermore, he knew from the outset that the Israelites would not heed the heavy warnings he was sent to deliver. Where did Isaiah get his authority, his confidence and courage, to speak so strongly against his own people, God's chosen ones? From God himself.

In the year that King Uzziah died, I saw the Lord seated on a throne, high and exalted, and the train of his robe filled the temple. Above him were seraphs, each with six wings: With two wings they covered their faces, with two they covered their feet, and with two they were flying. And they were calling to one another:

> "Holy, holy, holy is the LORD Almighty;
> the whole earth is full of his glory."

At the sound of their voices the doorposts and thresholds shook and the temple was filled with smoke.

"Woe to me!" I cried. "I am ruined! For I am a man of unclean lips, and I live among a people of unclean lips, and my eyes have seen the King, the LORD Almighty."

Then one of the seraphs flew to me with a live coal in his hand, which he had taken with tongs from the altar. With it he touched my mouth and said, "See, this has touched your lips; your guilt is taken away and your sin atoned for."

Then I heard the voice of the Lord saying, "Whom shall I send? And who will go for us?"

And I said, "Here am I [*Henani*]. Send me!"
He said, "Go, and tell this people:
" 'Be ever hearing, but never understanding;
be ever seeing, but never perceiving.'
Make the heart of this people calloused;
make their ears dull and close their eyes.
Otherwise they might see with their eyes,
hear with their ears,
understand with their hearts,
and turn and be healed."
Then I said, "For how long, O Lord?"
And he answered:
"Until the cities lie ruined and without inhabitant,
until the houses are left deserted and the fields ruined and ravaged,
until the LORD has sent everyone far away and the land is utterly forsaken.
And though a tenth remains in the land, it will again be laid waste.
But as the terebinth and oak leave stumps when they are cut down,
so the holy seed will be the stump in the land" (Isa. 6:1–13).

When we think of God's great prophets, whether in the Bible or throughout human history, we expect them to be individuals of strong character, somehow worthy of the honor, truly holy men and women of God. If they do find themselves prone to pangs of inadequacy or doubt, they should keep these feelings to themselves, so that the force of God's message is not diluted by their own human weaknesses. When we find Isaiah, the greatest prophet of all, crying out that he is undone (KJV), we ordinary mortals might well ask how we can have any hope at all, either for ourselves or for the power of the testimony we want to have for the Lord.

Fortunately, the answer lies in Isaiah 6, where we observe the sudden change in Isaiah from his "woe" to his "go." The whole passage expresses the reality of his direct meeting with God. It was not merely a vision or a secondary manifestation: Isaiah actually saw God with his eyes and heard God's voice. This encounter is different from others in our study; in them God initiated contact by calling on a particular person, who in turn chose whether or not to respond. Here, God asked himself a rhetorical question, "Whom shall I send? And who will go for us?" It was up to Isaiah to volunteer for the mission, which he did with great gusto, even though only a moment before he was writhing in moral agony.

It was not merely the certain presence of God appearing before him with shaking and smoke that mobilized Isaiah's mouth. While he would need these sensational memories to sustain him through many years, God's authority and power were more tangibly demonstrated to Isaiah: the coal from the altar touched his lips.

The altar was the place of ritual sacrifice, to which an individual brought offerings in acknowledgment of sins and received God's forgiveness. The altar was also a place of thanksgiving and praise. But the altar played a different, quite unique role in Isaiah's scene. No sacrifice occurred, in the sense of an animal being killed and offered up to God by the prophet. Instead, a seraph took a live coal from the altar fire and applied it to Isaiah's lips, a unilateral gesture of complete healing and acceptance, accomplished in the place where God's presence was most highly concentrated.

Fire conveys multiple meanings in the Bible. It is a powerful force of destruction and judgment (Gen. 19:24–29); but it is also an agent of refining and purifying (Zech. 13:9). Thirdly, fire represents the power and presence of God. When God led Israel during the Exodus, he guided and comforted them by a visible sign (Exod. 13:21). When Elijah challenged the prophets of Baal to prove the power of their false god, God provided fire in abundance (1 Kings 18:38–39). Hebrews 12:29 quotes Deuteronomy 4:24, "God is a consuming fire." Though we come with awe, we need not fear; God has demonstrated his acceptance of our offering by giving "himself up for us as a fragrant offering and sacrifice to God" (Eph. 5:2).

At some time or other you have probably burned your tongue trying to drink or eat something too hot. Whether you spat out the mouthful or swallowed it, the damage was done; your enjoyment of the rest of the meal was ruined. Can you imagine, then, the excruciating pain caused by the coal on Isaiah's lips, the body part most sensitive to temperature? Yet he did not even mention the physical agony. It was not the searing but the spiritual sealing for service that was significant at that moment. What mattered most was the unforgettable sensory imprint of his experience: God had touched his lips and his life directly, and there was no refuting or running away from that reality. From then on, as he wrote the remaining sixty chapters over the course of perhaps as many years, Isaiah spoke with the full authority of God.

What is it that you want to say, with your lips and with your life? In what ways has God authorized and empowered you to speak for him? Are you careful to base your words on your own unshakable experience, and not on vicarious visions?

Purity

The hot coal from the altar did more than establish Isaiah's authority as God's prophet. Remember the seraph's words "See, this has touched your lips; your guilt is taken away and your sin atoned for" (Isa. 6:7). Perhaps you are wondering, What guilt? What sin? And how did the coal remove them?

Isaiah was obviously distraught over having seen God face to face, an act which, he knew, was punishable by death (Exod. 33:20). Moreover, he was troubled by his state of uncleanness. We can look at this word in at least four ways, all of which may have been on Isaiah's mind. First, he began his book of prophecy "in the year Uzziah died." As a Jew, Isaiah knew that contact with a dead body made him ritually unclean (Num. 19). Worse, Uzziah had leprosy (the Hebrew word was used for various skin diseases), which made him ceremonially unclean and also necessitated his exclusion from both the temple and the capital city (Num. 12:14–15; 2 Chron. 26:21). Either of these physical conditions may have added to Isaiah's sense of discomfort and defilement in God's presence.

But the permanent, pervading reason for Isaiah's distress was his recognition of sinfulness, his own and his people's: "For I am a man of unclean lips, and I live among a people of unclean lips" (Isa. 6:5). The chapter began with a three-fold ovation to God, "Holy, holy holy is the LORD Almighty" (v. 3). In the presence of his all-holy God, Isaiah was overcome with a sense of his own unrighteousness. Surely, God's absolute holiness both attracts and repels us—it offers our only hope, and yet it destroys all hope of redemption, since we humans can never deserve to approach it.

Have you struggled, as I have, with God's repeated command in the Bible, "Be holy, for I am holy" (Lev. 11:44; 19:2; 20:26; Rom. 12:1; Heb. 12:14; 1 Peter 1:15–16), knowing the cruel impossibility of the assignment (Ps. 53; Rom. 7)? Why would he expect us to achieve something of which we are incapable, we who are by definition flawed, fallen human beings?

Again we see the greatness of God and his word in drawing us to himself with his enabling power. Just as God provided the live coal from his holy altar to take away the guilt and atone for the sin of Isaiah, he offers to impute holiness to us through the accepted sacrifice of his son, Jesus. Rather than tormenting us with impossible demands for holiness, God has already fulfilled his promise to make us holy: "Then the LORD said to Moses, 'Say to the Israelites, "You must observe my Sabbaths. This will be a sign between me and you for the generations to come, so you may know that I am the LORD, who makes you holy"'" (Exod. 31:13); "Consecrate yourselves and be holy, because I am the LORD your God. Keep my decrees and follow them. I am the LORD, who makes you holy" (Lev. 20:7–8). As the writer of Hebrews explains, through Christ we have a new altar (13:10) and a more complete atonement (Chapter 9). Our hope is restored, for our holiness is achieved by God not at the altar but on the cross, if we will but accept his finished work by faith, as Isaiah did.

The fourth use of the word *unclean* refers to the dietary laws, or *Kashreth*. The Talmud specifies nearly 700 rules regarding what is and is not to be eaten, how it must be prepared, and how one is to live in purity. A simplistic explanation of these commands, which fill many chapters in Exodus, Leviticus, and Numbers, and even more volumes of commentary by subsequent rabbis, is that they provided protection by proscribing certain foods or food preparations that might have caused contamination and even death in that early desert culture, which was without modern methods of hygiene and refrigeration. More important from a spiritual standpoint, the dietary laws constituted a plumb line of righteousness by which obedience to God could be measured. In the last analysis, Jews have "kept kosher" not because the practice was healthy but because God commanded it.

In the New Testament, a very important scene for Gentile Christians occurred in the life of the apostle Peter. An undercurrent of dissension ran through the early church as to whether believers in Christ had to become Jewish converts first, all pagans being regarded as alien and unclean. Peter's vision in Acts 10, in which a voice commanded him to kill and eat animals that were patently unclean, caused him much wonderment. When the vision was repeated three times, with the words "Do not call anything impure that God has made clean" (Acts 10:15; 11:9), Peter came to understand that God was opening the way of faith to the Gentiles, without the prerequisite of Jewish conversion and circumcision. His actions in entering a pagan home and baptizing people in the name of Christ were called into question by the church leaders, but his explanation was irrefutable: God had made it clear that it was up to him alone to determine who was clean or unclean in his sight, and he had confirmed his decision by the sign of the Holy Spirit "on all who heard the message. The circumcized believers who had come with Peter were astonished that the gift of the Holy Spirit had been poured out even on the Gentiles. For they heard them speaking in tongues and praising God" (Acts 10:44–46).

What I am suggesting is a connection between Isaiah's self-condemnation, Peter's acceptance of God's expanded definition of clean to apply to believers of different backgrounds, and your own process of sanctification. Recognizing your unworthiness, but claiming the worthiness of the Lamb, Jesus (Rev. 5:9–10), are you prepared to stand up in faith and answer God's call? As with Isaiah and the Gentile converts, you, too, have the promised seal of the Holy Spirit to make your ministry fruitful: "And you also were included in Christ when you heard the word of truth, the gospel of your salvation. Having believed, you were marked in him with a seal, the promised Holy Spirit, who is a deposit guaranteeing our inheritance until the redemption of those who are God's possession—to the praise of his glory" (Eph. 1:13–14; *See also* Eph. 4:30).

From the moment Isaiah was told that his guilt and sin were removed by the live coal, he believed that it was so. He immediately ceased wallowing in his own unworthiness. He applied God's general call to himself and stepped forward with a bold, cleansed conscience and a resounding "*Henani!*" Modern Christian, can you follow Isaiah's example and accept the free gift of redemption that has already been bought for you at great cost? Without assuming a holier-than-thou attitude, will you allow God to impute the purity of Christ's sacrifice as the once-for-all covering for your sin, enabling you to approach boldly the throne of grace (Heb. 4:16)? Have you offered yourself for service joyfully, gratefully, humbly, and confidently?

Security

Did you find it remarkable that after the scene described in Isaiah 6, the prophet never again seemed to question his commission, nor felt the need to defend his claim that God had indeed appointed and anointed him? He devoted himself to the task of recording God's words as they were revealed to him, without undue apology or analysis.

Sometimes it helps, as we endeavor to grow in our Christian faith, if we can bring to mind a striking scene from our past, like a powerful conversion experience or a personal call from God. When we encounter times of difficulty, doubt, or disappointment, we find comfort in recalling previous highlights, moments when we were certain that God was carrying us and caring for us in a special way. Often in the Old Testament, an altar was built or a stone set up as a remembrance of God's promises. After a particular victory against the Philistines, for example, "Samuel took a stone and set it up between Mizpah and Shen. He named it Ebenezer [which means "stone of help"], saying, 'Thus far has the LORD helped us'" (1 Sam. 7:12). Every time the Israelites passed that place, Ebenezer reminded them of God's presence and power.

For Isaiah, the live coal from God's holy altar sealed and sustained his faith in God for his entire lifetime. Whether or not we can locate an "Ebenezer" in our life, a solid marker on which to carve the name and date of our past personal experiences of God's presence, does not seem to matter much when it comes to finding security in regard to our present or future circumstances, on earth or in heaven. We can spout the good Protestant doctrine "Once saved, always saved," but the glibness of our theology may not guarantee our daily sense of confidence or joy.

Isaiah's hope came not from a single event in his personal life, but from a continuous encounter with his personal God. It was the Lord's awesomely complex and beautiful character—his holiness, majesty, power, judgment, and love—that Isaiah set forth in the pages of his prophecy. Are your lips sealed for silence or for service? Are you reluctant to speak of your faith out of a sense of personal guilt and unworthiness? Christ *has* removed it, as surely as did Isaiah's altar coal, "as far as the east is from the west" (Ps. 103:11–12). Put on the robe of righteousness provided for you by your sinless Savior (Isa. 61:10). Are you intimidated by the world's rebellion against God and rejection of his messengers? Such is God's way, that only a remnant will be redeemed. Christ has given to you and to me the same authority and command God gave to Isaiah, to "go and tell this people" (compare Isa. 6:9 with Matt. 28:18–20). Can you grab hold of his promises with both passion and patience, as you wait eagerly for eternity?

> In that day you will say:
>   "I will praise you, O LORD.
> Although you were angry with me,
> your anger has turned away
>   and you have comforted me.
> Surely God is my salvation;
>   I will trust and not be afraid.
> The LORD, the LORD, is my strength and my song;
>   he has become my salvation."
> With joy you will draw water
>   from the wells of salvation.
>   In that day you will say:
> "Give thanks to the LORD, call on his name;
>   make known among the nations what he has done,
>   and proclaim that his name is exalted.
> Sing to the LORD for he has done glorious things;
>   let this be known to all the world.

Shout aloud and sing for joy, people of Zion,
    for great is the Holy One of Israel among you" (Isa. 12:1–6).

The salvation, the strength, and the song came from the LORD, the Holy One of Israel. The greatness and the glory are his. The authority and the ability to speak, serve, and live acceptably in his sight are his gifts as well. Rest securely in his love and sing joyfully as you draw upon and share the water of salvation.

Hark the voice of Jesus calling, "Who will go and work today?
Fields are white, and harvests waiting, who will bear the sheaves
    away?"
Loud and long the Master calleth, rich reward he offers thee;
Who will answer, gladly saying, "Here am I; send me, send me"?

If you cannot be the watchman standing high on Zion's wall,
Pointing out the path to heaven, offering life and peace to all,
If you cannot speak like angels, if you cannot preach like Paul,
You can tell the love of Jesus, you can say, "He died for all."

Let none hear you idly saying, "There is nothing I can do,"
While the souls of men are dying, and the Master calls for you:
Take the task he gives you gladly; let his work your pleasure be;
Answer quickly when he calleth, "Here am I; send me, send
    me."

Daniel March, 1868

11

Ananias
The Simplicity of Self

Primary Scripture Readings

Acts 9 and 22

Supplementary References

1 Samuel 9	Matthew 7:7
1 Kings 17	Mark 9:24
Jonah	Hebrews 6:19

Questions for Study and Discussion

1. Read the two passages about Ananias of Damascus. How much time elapsed between the two accounts? From whose point of view was each one written? What similarities and differences do you notice?

2. Compare the behaviors of Saul and Ananias. What was each man doing before God interrupted him? How did God get the attention of each? What did God say? How did they respond? What permanent impact did these events have on each of their lives?

3. What other instances can you think of from the Bible in which two individuals are each directed to expect to meet or find the other? What do such passages suggest to you about how God works through human affairs?

4. What attitudes are reflected in Ananias's response to God's call, both before and after he heard exactly what God wanted him to do?

5. How can you recognize God's voice, especially if he were to direct you to take some unusual or even dangerous action?

6. When Ananias entered the room where Saul was waiting, what, do you think, was going on in each man's mind and heart? From Acts 9 and

22, reconstruct their conversation, including any thoughts they might have had as "asides."

The last man in our study is Ananias, and for his story we must go to the New Testament to Acts 9. It is not as large a leap from the Old Testament as you may imagine, however, since his name, his words, and his actions are simply Greek equivalents of the same character traits we have been exploring in the Old Testament. Ananias is the same name as Hananiah in Hebrew, which means "The Lord is gracious." His response in Greek was *Paristano*,[1] which carries the same intent and range of meanings as the Hebrew *Henani*.

While the focus of this study will be Ananias, it is clear that the central figure in Acts 9 is Saul of Tarsus, who was confronted by the risen Christ on the road to Damascus. Let us recall this life-changing and indeed world-changing episode:

> Meanwhile, Saul was still breathing out murderous threats against the Lord's disciples. He went to the high priest and asked him for letters to the synagogues in Damascus, so that if he found any there who belonged to the Way, whether men or women, he might take them as prisoners to Jerusalem. As he neared Damascus on his journey, suddenly a light from heaven flashed around him. He fell to the ground and heard a voice say to him, "Saul, Saul, why do you persecute me?"
>
> "Who are you, Lord?" Saul asked.
>
> "I am Jesus, whom you are persecuting," he replied. "Now

---

1. *Strong's Exhaustive Concordance* (Grand Rapids: Baker Book House, rep. 1987) gives these possible meanings of this verb, depending on context: "(trans.) to stand beside, to exhibit, proffer, recommend, substantiate; or (intrans.) to be at hand (ready), aid; assist, bring before, command, commend, give presently, present, prove, provide, shew, stand (before, by, here, up, with), yield." The KJV chooses "Behold, I am here, Lord," with the "I am here" in italics to indicate the figurative addition. The NIV expresses it simply as "Yes, Lord." We found both of these to be common translations of *Henani* in the Old Testament.

get up and go into the city, and you will be told what you must do."

The men traveling with Saul stood there speechless; they heard the sound but did not see anyone. Saul got up from the ground, but when he opened his eyes he could see nothing. So they led him by the hand into Damascus. For three days he was blind, and did not eat or drink anything (Acts 9:1–9).

There are several important points to notice in this passage. First, it really was Christ, not just a vision, who appeared to Saul. Second, there were physical manifestations of the visitation—the sound of his voice and the flash of light—that those traveling with Saul also sensed but could not identify. Saul was struck blind and had to be led by the hand into Damascus, where he waited three days without eating or drinking. He was not idle during that time, however. He had quite a bit of thinking to do, and praying. And God offered him some comfort while he waited.

In Damascus there was a disciple named Ananias. The Lord called to him in a vision. "Ananias!"

"Yes, Lord [*Paristano*]," he answered.

The Lord told him, "Go to the house of Judas on Straight Street and ask for a man from Tarsus named Saul, for he is praying. In a vision he has seen a man named Ananias come and place his hands on him to restore his sight."

"Lord," Ananias answered, "I have heard many reports about this man and all the harm he has done to your saints in Jerusalem. And he has come here with authority from the chief priests to arrest all who call on your name."

But the Lord said to Ananias, "Go! This man is my chosen instrument to carry my name before the Gentiles and their kings and before the people of Israel. I will show him how much he must suffer for my name."

Then Ananias went to the house and entered it. Placing his hands on Saul, he said, "Brother Saul, the Lord—Jesus, who appeared to you on the road as you were coming here—has sent me so that you may see again and be filled with the Holy Spirit." Immediately, something like scales fell from Saul's eyes, and he

147

could see again. He got up and was baptized, and after taking some food, he regained his strength (Acts 9:10–19).

Caution

When God called to Ananias in a vision, he answered simply, "Yes, Lord." There is no indication of shock, or even surprise at the fact that God called him by name in this way. The calm ordinariness of this exchange is in sharp contrast to the terror and turmoil we noticed in Saul's initial encounter with the Lord, suggesting that it was not as unusual an event. As Hebrews 11:6 points out, "Without faith it is impossible to please God, because anyone who comes to him must believe that he exists and that he rewards those who earnestly seek him." Ananias had an ongoing relationship with God—there was already a context for communication. It is even reasonable to conceive that Ananias was in the act of praying for the protection of the believers in Damascus when God appeared before him. If this is true, why should he have been surprised that God would manifest himself by way of answering that prayer? As you consider the obvious thrust of this question, ask yourself how often you pray, earnestly seeking him, but not really believing that he has heard and will supply your need.

If God's appearance to Ananias was not so unusual, his instructions certainly were extraordinary: "Go to the house of Judas on Straight Street and ask for a man from Tarsus named Saul, for he is praying" (Acts 9:11). The fact that God would be in the least concerned for Saul, rather than striking him dead for hurting the church, was surely not the sort of answer Ananias was expecting. Worse yet, God wanted Ananias to risk his life to minister to this known enemy! How could God care more for evil Saul than for faithful Ananias? Whose prayers counted more, anyway? Did God really know what he was doing?

What I find encouraging about Ananias's response to God's words is not only the fact that he offered himself willingly *before* he knew the mission for which he was called, but also that afterward he reacted first with honesty to express his concerns and then with faith to carry out his assignment without fear. Notice that Ananias did not whine or complain, "Why me? What have I done to deserve death at the hands of this madman?" Nor did he argue against God's orders or suggest a better plan. He asked no questions at all, but merely reported the news he had heard about the man to whom God was sending him. He said simply, "Lord, I have heard many reports about this man and all the harm he has done to your saints in Jerusalem. And he has come here with authority from the chief priests to arrest all who call on your name" (vv. 13–14).

In telling God what he knew about Saul, Ananias was not implying that he knew more than God did about Saul's avid persecution of the church. The straightforward declarative tone in which Ananias offered his information reflected an attitude of reverence that allowed God to unfold the major turn of events in which Ananias himself was about to become involved: "Go! This man is my chosen instrument to carry my name before the Gentiles and their kings and before the people of Israel. I will show him how much he must suffer for my name" (vv. 15–16).

Ananias did not resist God's orders by posing more questions; he simply expressed his concerns from his own human vantage point, and then was satisfied by the revelation of God's greater perspective. In this way he was privileged to play an important role in the completion of Saul's transformation from persecutor to apostle of the church. As God showed him the scope of these far-reaching changes, Ananias's immediate concerns were more than adequately answered; his caution gave way to action, and without another word he set his feet in the direction of Straight Street.

Never be shy about going to God with your honest concerns. Tell him what you know and what you need to know. Confess your doubts as well as your faith (see Mark 9:24). "Ask and it will be given to you" (Matt. 7:7), Jesus said, meaning that we can list things we want, but also that God is waiting to supply the comfort we need by giving us assurances of his plan and an answer for every question. But consider this: How do you conceive of answered prayer? Are you eagerly expecting that God will fit into your mold and move the cosmos in accordance with your conception of the way it should be? Or are you prepared to yield your understanding and your very life to participate in his surprising plan?

Confirming Coincidences

God sent Ananias to Saul, and Ananias went. Meanwhile, God told Saul to expect Ananias. Both in the original account in Acts 9 and in Paul's retelling in Acts 22, the fact that each was directed to the other is made clear. When the two came together in Judas's house, each was already prepared to accept the other as sent from God. We could call such a meeting a miracle of the mundane. Yet there is always reason to be amazed as we contemplate God's orchestrating the ordinary temporal events to accomplish his eternal purposes and to make his people aware of his presence.

Why did God reveal himself to Saul in the fullness of his personal glory on the road outside of Damascus, and then work through the agency of his human servant once Saul was inside the city? To appreciate this phenomenon and the role we can play as ministers of God's word, imagine what might have occurred had Ananias not shown up at Judas's door to restore Saul's sight. In that case, one small detail of Christ's instructions would not have been exactly fulfilled. Knowing, as he did, that the test of a true prophet was determined by whether his claims in the name of the Lord were literally brought to pass (Deut. 18:22), Saul could have called into question the identity and validity of the one who had spoken to him, Jesus himself. He would then have begun to regard the incident in a somewhat lesser light than the full flash from heaven it actually was. Since those around him could not confirm the full content of the revelation, and since the subsequent events Jesus foretold had not yet occurred, it would have been natural for Saul to become dubious of his own experience. He might have thought, "Well, I guess I was wrong. It must have been just an incredible stroke of lightning that affected my eyes and ears for a while. A lucky escape from a natural disaster, but not a revelation from God, since what happened later didn't exactly fit what I had been told. Now, about those followers of the Way. . . ."

Instead, the fact that Ananias did arrive as God's promised human agent confirmed the reality of Saul's confrontation by the living Christ and sealed his conversion: Christ was indeed the Son of God, whose followers he had been persecuting but who now washed away his sins and set him on a new course to change other lives with the dramatic message of resurrection power.

Now consider the scene of Saul's restoration from Ananias's viewpoint. Although he had initially expressed wonder at why God would send him into the hands of an enemy, it was through his own hands that God completed the healing process that transformed Paul into the world's greatest evangelist. While in studying this passage we tend to concentrate on the "Damascus Road spectacle," we ought not to miss the significance of this "Straight Street miracle," in which the lives of Saul and Ananias converged to demonstrate both the power and the grace of God. For these two it was not merely a chance connection but part of the purposeful plan for the fulfillment of faith in each.

Three interesting passages in the Old Testament bear study, for they shed light on this matter of how God works on the human plane to bring people and circumstances together. On the one hand, he brought Saul to Samuel and told Samuel to anoint him king (1 Sam. 9). And after God had ravens bring food to Elijah during a famine in Israel, he then sent the prophet to Zarephath, where God "prepared a widow" to care for him with food he himself miraculously provided, to their mutual blessing (see 1 Kings 17). On the other hand, after God commanded Jonah to preach against Nineveh, that prophet seemed to find convenient confirming circumstances that made him think he could avoid the task. We must examine our interpretation of seeming coincidences as guidelines for our lives along with careful consideration of God's other means of revelation: study of his Word, prayer, and consultation with other believers.

Suppose someone told you to go jump in the lake. Would you do it? Suppose God told you to jump in the lake. How would you differentiate his voice from the devil's, or decide whether the notion was just a figment of your imagination? What if, when you got to the lake, there was a person drowning whom you were able to rescue, and who then told you that God had sent you (by name) to save him? As you begin to look for patterns in the fabric of God's handiwork, you will be amazed to discover ways in which the "warp" of your actions crosses the "woof" of other lives, for your mutual enrichment and encouragement. Although God grants each human the freedom of independent choice—we are not mere puppets—the outcome is far from random. As with Ananias and Saul, God weaves multiple strands together to accomplish his plan for each.

Sometimes God works in cataclysmic ways, like drying up the Red Sea, or causing the sun to stand still. At other times, we see his hands working more gently. There is another beautiful touch in the story of Ananias's visit to Saul—the human touch. Not only did Ananias attest to the reality of Christ's revelation as the almighty God; he also through his personal experience claimed Christ as the Son of Man, who shares in all the joys and pains of our humanity and appreciates our need for physical closeness: "Then Ananias went to the house and entered it. *Placing his hands on Saul,* he said, 'Brother Saul, the Lord—Jesus, who appeared to you on the road as you were coming here—has sent me so that you may see again and be filled with the Holy Spirit'" (Acts 9:17, italics added).

Are you "touchy" about being touched? How is God using you to touch the lives of others? We know almost nothing about this man Ananias apart from his willingness to administer to Saul the healing power of God at a crucial moment. This simple act of obedience did more than restore Paul's vision; it led Paul immediately to the next step of baptism, even before he had anything to eat after his three-day fast (Acts 9:19). It provided an anchor to Paul's faith, firm and secure (Heb. 6:19), to which he clung for support and on which he hung his claim as an apostle. Thus, we do indeed see the graciousness of God in allowing Ananias to play a small but significant part in the events that changed the course of Paul's life and of world history. When God calls you to serve him, even if he asks for only a simple, seemingly insignificant gesture, pray that you will respond honestly and without hesitation.

> Lord, speak to me, that I may speak
> In living echoes of thy tone;
> As thou hast sought, so let me seek
> Thy erring children lost and lone.
>
> O lead me, Lord, that I may lead
> The wandering and the wavering feet;
> O feed me, Lord, that I may feed
> Thy hungering ones with manna sweet!
>
> O teach me, Lord, that I may teach
> The precious things thou dost impart;
> And wing my words that they may reach
> The hidden depths of many a heart.
>
> O fill me with thy fullness, Lord,
> Until my very heart o'erflow
> In kindling thought and glowing word
> Thy love to tell, thy praise to show.
>
> O use me, Lord, use even me,
> Just as thou wilt and when and where;
> Until thy blessed face I see,
> Thy rest, thy joy, thy glory share.
>
> Frances R. Havergal, 1872

12

Jehovah and Jesus
The Sovereign Selves

Primary Scripture Readings

Isaiah 58; 59:1–2; 65:1–5
Psalm 40:6–8
John 7:3–9; 8; 14; 16:12–15
Hebrews 10:5–7; 12:1–3

Jeremiah 29:10–14; 33:2–9
Proverb 1:22–33
Revelation 3:20
Philippians 2:5–11

Supplementary References

Exodus 3:14
Deuteronomy 4:29; 32:18–21
Isaiah 30:18–19
Psalm 50:7, 14–15; 91:14–16; 145:18
Jeremiah 31:31–37
Zechariah 8:8; 13:9
Romans 8:28–30; 10:12–13
James 4:8

Questions for Study and Discussion

1. Consider how God responded to the particular spiritual and physical needs of each of the men in this book. In what ways did his response depend on their attitudes and actions?

2. How did God reveal himself and his will to each of these men? In what ways did he express different aspects of his own character as he dealt with them?

3. From the passages listed above, describe the circumstances under which God said *Henani.* Does he say it today? When and why does he not always seem responsive to his people? When you turn to God in prayer, how can you be sure he will listen?

4. Under what circumstances did Christ (the Son of God, Jesus) say *Henani*? To whom? Why? How does his response help you?

5. In what ways, do you think, does the Holy Spirit express the idea of *Henani*? Write down any verses you can find that describe his role in relation to Jehovah and Jesus, and in relation to believers today. How could he help you to respond to God's call?

6. What questions remain in your mind about God, the Bible, and your own walk of faith? Write them down now, determine a course of study, and form a small group to join your search for answers as you continue to grow.

G od calling yet," moans an old tent meeting tear-jerker. Unlike the investment firm that claims it gets immediate attention whenever it speaks, God's patience must be longsuffering indeed, as his messages of warning and promise so often seem to fall on deaf ears and hard hearts. The Bible informs us that he holds the future of the universe, which he created, in his hands, but that only a few souls, a tattered remnant at that, will eventually respond to his offer of eternity.

Our study has brought us into contact with ten men in the Scriptures who were called by God and who responded in various ways. Although their *Henanis* provided a thread of commonality among them, we were able to identify markedly different aspects of their personalities, and of the character of God, as we studied their lives. Hopefully, you have gained insights into your own attitudes and actions in response to God's personal invitation, which we shall examine in the final chapter.

But first let us consider God's role. More than just rapping his knuckles raw on the cold, hard doors of human hearts, he actively demonstrates his open, willing attitude of commitment and availability when his people cry out to him in need. Not only does he command and deserve our complete devotion, but he also evokes it by his own generous example. He, too, has said

Henani, in his Word, both as the Father and the Son—Jehovah and Jesus.

Jehovah

Recently, my husband performed at a benefit concert to raise money for a hospital in Jerusalem. While we waited for the overture to begin, my children observed two distinctive features of the occasion. Nearly all the men in the audience wore yarmulkes, and the program notes offered thanks to God for his blessing but omitted the vowel in spelling his name: G-d. Both customs were explainable by the fact that the audience was made up almost entirely of Orthodox Jews, who consider the name of God to be too holy to be written down or spoken casually, lest it become a graven image or be taken in vain in violation of the Ten Commandments.

We have noticed the importance of names in the Bible. They express a significant aspect of a person or place; renaming represents a new relationship or direction. In our culture, we tend to be aware of the meaning of names only when we are choosing them for our children, and even then our decision is based largely on the sound of the word when spoken in conjunction with the family name (the middle name usually being omitted except in moments of anger). When we hear a name that has an obvious meaning in current usage, we tend to smile at its quaint or ethnic quality—Blue Moon Odom, Meadowlark Lemon, or Crazy Horse, for example. The Pilgrims, Quakers, and other special religious groups often gave their children names with recognizable meanings in English—Oceanus, Remember, Humility, etc. But in the 1970s, people smirked when singers Sonny and Cher named their daughter Chastity.

A name is an identity, a specificity, "this one and no other," but it also provides a point of connection with someone or something else. God is God alone—there is nothing and no one with whom to compare or describe him. He is his own terms, the only pure essence. When Moses pleaded to know the name of

157

the one sending him to deliver Israel, God wasn't just being cute when he answered, "I AM WHO I AM. This is what you are to say to the Israelites: 'I AM has sent me to you'" (Exod. 3:14). This name of God is so holy that it was represented in the text by a sort of unutterable code, four consonants referred to as the Tetragrammaton YHWH, which was transliterated as "Jehovah," but for which the original pronunciation has long been lost in the secrecy of antiquity. When this word is found in the text, the more common name *Adonai* is read, and translated into English as "LORD," written in capital letters to distinguish it from instances in which *Adonai* is used and written simply as Lord.

As we have studied the characters of these men in the Scriptures, we have embarked on a search for our own identities, trying to answer the question, "Who am I?" for ourselves, and recognizing the significance of our relationship with our maker and redeemer as the essential consideration for our quest. Now we come to apply that question to God: Who does he say he is, or claim to be? From his own perspective, how does he handle the issue, "Who am I?" His answer is both majestic and mysterious: "I AM WHO I AM."

Even though God is incomparable and complete within himself, he still desires to draw us into a personal relationship by promising to answer when we call, to fulfill his will for our development. This is not to say that we have only to snap our fingers for God to jump into action on our behalf, nor that there is a magic formula for "successful" prayer, if we define success in terms of getting whatever we think we want from the "good giver."

Let us now turn to some of the most powerful expressions of God's essential character in the Bible, and try to uncover the basic requirements for eliciting his *Henani* response.

> "Hear, O my people, and I will speak,
>   O Israel, and I will testify against you:
>   I am God, your God. . . .
> Sacrifice thank offerings to God,
>   fulfill your vows to the most High,

and call upon me in the day of trouble;
   I will deliver you, and you will honor me"
      (Ps. 50:7, 14–15).

Yet the LORD longs to be gracious to you;
   he rises to show you compassion.
For the LORD is a God of justice.
   Blessed are all who wait for him!

O people of Zion, who live in Jerusalem, you will weep no
   more. How gracious he will be when you cry for help! As
   soon as he hears, he will answer you" (Isa. 30:18–19).

"Shout it aloud, do not hold back.
   Raise your voice like a trumpet.
Declare to my people their rebellion
   and to the house of Jacob their sins.
For day after day they seek me out;
   they seem eager to know my ways,
as if they were a nation that does what is right
   and has not forsaken the commands of its God.
Then your light will break forth like the dawn,
   and your healing will quickly appear;
then your righteousness will go before you,
and the glory of the LORD will be your rear guard.
Then you will call, and the LORD will answer;
   you will cry for help, and he will say: "Here am I [Henani]."

"If you keep your feet from breaking the Sabbath
   and from doing as you please on my holy day,
if you call the Sabbath a delight
   and the LORD's day honorable,
and if you honor it by not going your own way
   and not doing as you please or speaking idle words,
then you will find your joy in the LORD.
   and I will cause you to ride on the heights of the land
   and to feast on the inheritance of your father Jacob."
The mouth of the LORD has spoken (Isa. 58:1–2, 8–9, 13–14).

"How long will you simple ones love your simple ways?
    How long will mockers delight in mockery
    and fools hate knowledge?
If you had responded to my rebuke,
    I would have poured out my heart to you
    and made my thoughts known to you.
But since you rejected me when I called
    and no one gave heed when I stretched out my hand,
since you ignored all my advice
    and would not accept my rebuke,
I in turn will laugh at your disaster;
    I will mock when calamity overtakes you—
when calamity overtakes you like a storm,
    when disaster sweeps over you like a whirlwind,
    when distress and troubles overwhelm you.

"Then they will call to me but I will not answer;
    they will look for me but will not find me.
Since they hated knowledge
    and did not choose to fear the LORD,
since they would not accept my advice
    and spurned my rebuke,
they will eat the fruit of their ways
    and be filled with the fruit of their schemes.
For the waywardness of the simple will kill them,
    and the complacency of fools will destroy them;
but whoever listens to me will live in safety
    and be at ease, without fear of harm" (Prov. 1:22–33).

This is what the LORD says, he who made the earth, the LORD
    who formed it and established it—the LORD is his name:
    "Call to me and I will answer you and tell you great and
    unsearchable things you do not know" (Jer. 33:2).

This is what the LORD says: "When seventy years are com-
    pleted for Babylon, I will come to you and fulfill my gra-
    cious promise to bring you back to this place. For I know
    the plans I have for you," declares the LORD, "plans to
    prosper you and not to harm you, plans to give you hope

and a future. Then you will call upon me and come to pray to me, and I will listen to you. You will seek me and find me when you seek me with all your heart. I will be found by you," declares the LORD, "and will bring you back from captivity. I will gather you from all the nations and places where I have banished you," declares the LORD, "and will bring you back to the place from which I carried you into exile" (Jer. 29:10–14).

> Seek the LORD while he may be found;
> call on him while he is near (Isa. 55:6).

Does God always answer our prayers? Is he always "nice" to us? Is he always waiting around, just hoping we will call, so he can shower us with blessings? Or are there conditions to his unconditional love? Do you find in these passages confusing or contradictory information about what God will or will not do for his people? Why?

As we look carefully at these and many other passages, several important guidelines begin to emerge: (1) God is sovereign—he knows the future and he knows our hearts. He is not only aware but also in control of all things: (2) God is omnipotent and omnipresent—there is nothing too hard for him, no place he cannot go to find and bring us back: (3) God's promise to respond is predicated on our initiative—he does not break us to his will, but waits for us to come to him, realizing our need. Only when we come can he truly bless us with abundance; only then can he use us as true servants. He hides his face from us when we have turned away from him, but when we seek him, he will be found.

Jesus

Jesus' own *Henani* in response to his father serves as our best example and encouragement:

> Your attitude should be the same as that of Christ Jesus: who
> being in very nature God,
> did not consider equality with God something to be grasped,

161

> but made himself nothing,
>> taking the very nature of a servant,
>> being made in human likeness,
> And being found in appearance as a man,
>> he humbled himself
>> and became obedient to death—
>>> even death on a cross!
> Therefore God exalted him to the highest place
>> and gave him the name that is above every name,
> that at the name of Jesus every knee should bow,
>> in heaven and on earth and under the earth,
> and every tongue confess that Jesus Christ is Lord,
>> to the glory of God the Father (Phil. 2:5–11).

After running through the roster of Old Testament saints, the writer of Hebrews adds Christ to the list of those who submitted to God's service:

> Therefore, since we are surrounded by such a great cloud of witnesses, let us throw off everything that hinders and the sin that so easily entangles, and let us run with perseverance the race marked out for us. Let us fix our eyes on Jesus, the author and perfecter of our faith, who for the joy set before him endured the cross, scorning its shame, and sat down at the right hand of the throne of God. Consider him who endured such opposition from sinful men, so that you will not grow weary and lose heart (Heb. 12:1–3).

In addition to Jesus' serving as our model for willing service, we need also to notice his words, in which he repeatedly affirmed his identity wth God. Throughout the Book of John, we find Jesus making statements about who he is: "I am the bread of life (6:35, 48) . . . the light of the world (8:12; 9:5) . . . the gate (10:7, 9) . . . the good shepherd (10:11) . . . the resurrection and the life (11:25) . . . the vine (15:5)." He consistently explained to the disciples that not only was he sent by God, but also he was one with God. More powerful was his threefold "I am," when he stepped forward to face the soldiers in Gethsemane (John 18). Perhaps his clearest self-definition came in John 8, when the

Jews attempted to stone him because they rightly understood he was claiming to be God himself when he said, "I tell you the truth, before Abraham was born, I am!" (John 8:58).

Again in Hebrews, we find Psalm 40 quoted and used to elaborate on the significance of Christ's sacrifice:

> Therefore, when Christ came into the world, he said:
> "Sacrifice and offering you did not desire,
>   but a body you prepared for me:
> with burnt offerings and sin offerings you were not pleased.
>
> Then I said, "Here I am" ([*Henani*]—NIV)—it is written about me in the scroll—
>   I have come to do your will, O God."
> First he said, "Sacrifices and offerings, burnt offerings and sin offerings you did not desire, nor were you pleased with them" (although the law required them to be made). Then he said, "Here I am, I have come to do your will." He sets aside the first to establish the second. And by that will, we have been made holy through the sacrifice of the body of Jesus Christ once for all (Heb. 10:5–10).

Joy

At the dedication of the Temple in Jerusalem, Solomon prayed for God's blessing on Israel. Not just in case but *when* they rebelled, bringing on themselves every kind of disaster—crime, famine, drought, war, plague, exile—Solomon besought God to hear, forgive, and restore the people at the time they would turn back to him with sincere hearts acknowledging their sin. In every case, God promised to answer when called on in the right way: "If my people, who are called by my name, will humble themselves and pray and seek my face and turn from their wicked ways, then I will hear from heaven and will forgive their sin and will heal their land" (2 Chron. 7:14). In the New Testament, James said,

> Submit yourselves, then, to God. Resist the devil, and he will flee from you. Come near to God and he will come near to you.

163

Wash your hands, you sinners, and purify your hearts, you double-minded. Grieve, mourn and wail. Change your laughter to mourning and your joy to gloom. Humble yourselves before the LORD, and he will lift you up (James 4:7–10).

Isaiah promised "a crown of beauty instead of ashes, the oil of gladness instead of mourning, and a garment of praise instead of a spirit of despair" (Isa. 61:3). In the last days, "the ransomed of the LORD will return. They will enter Zion with singing; everlasting joy will crown their heads. Gladness and joy will overtake them, and sorrow and sighing will flee away" (Isa. 35:10). Jesus said that he came that we might have life, and have it more abundantly (John 10:10). He also said, "As the Father has loved me, so have I loved you. Now remain in my love. If you obey my commands, you will remain in my love, just as I have obeyed my Father's commands and remain in his love. I have told you this so that my joy may be in you and that your joy may be complete" (John 15:9–11).

When he went to the Father, Jesus left that joy and love on earth in the form of the Holy Spirit, the third person of the Trinity. The Spirit teaches us everything about God and Christ, establishes our faith, and brings us comfort and strength as the Paraclete—the one who comes alongside to help. He has no ambition of his own, but desires only to glorify the Father and the Son. His testimony and total function could be summarized in the term *Henani,* as he makes himself available everywhere to communicate God's will. It is he who makes it possible for us to hear and respond to God's call as well.

Henani expresses the availability of God to his people—he is here, "God with us"—in every circumstance. It expresses his eternity—the timeless, present "Am." And it expresses his individuality and personality—not a formless force in a random universe but a real "I." When God says, "Here am I," he means every syllable, reaching out to welcome you into fellowship with him. God has said and will say *Henani* whenever you say *Henani* and mean it. What do you say?

Sing praise to God who reigns above, the God of all creation,
The God of power, the God of love, the God of our salvation;
With healing balm my soul he fills, and every faithless murmur
stills:
To God all praise and glory.

What God's almighty power hath made his gracious mercy keep-
eth;
By morning glow or evening shade his watchful eye ne'er sleep-
eth;
Within the kingdom of his might, Lo! all is just and all is right;
To God all praise and glory.

The Lord is never far away, but through all grief distressing,
An everpresent help and stay, our peace, and joy, and blessing;
As with a mother's tender hand, he leads his own, his chosen
band:
To God all praise and glory.

Thus all my gladsome way along, I sing aloud thy praises,
That men may hear the grateful song my voice unwearied raises;
Be joyful in the Lord, my heart, both soul and body bear your
part:
To God all praise and glory.

Johann J. Schütz, 1675
Trans. by Frances E. Cox, 1864

13

You
The Summoned Self

Primary Scripture Readings

Deuteronomy 11:18–21
Psalm 121
John 15:15–20
Hebrews 3:1–6
2 Corinthians 4:16–18
Revelation 17:14

Supplementary References

2 Chronicles 16:9
Psalm 34:8
Isaiah 46:8–10
Amos 9:4
Matthew 22:14

Mark 13:20
Luke 23:3–5
John 10:28; 13:18
Acts 10:41
1 Peter 2:4, 9

Questions for Study and Discussion

1. Use the following chart to review the lives and personalities of five or six of the characters in this study. What changes occurred over the course of their lives? What warnings and encouragements do they represent to you?

Name	Changes in Circumstances	Changes in Character	Lessons for My Life

_____

_____

_____

2. Which character study did you find most interesting? Write down and try to memorize any verses or examples that were especially comforting or challenging to you.

3. What have you learned about God's character and the ways he calls individuals to his service? Does he use other means today than in Bible times? How has he gotten your attention? How are you responding?

4. In what ways have you become sensitive to God's call? What is he inviting you to do with him? What costs or risks are involved? What benefits or blessings do you anticipate will come by accepting?

5. What have you learned through this study about reading and understanding the Bible for yourself? In what ways did your group format enrich your experience? Discuss ways to make your study and discussion time more valuable to yourself and others.

6. Each chapter has ended with a traditional hymn. Suggest another favorite hymn or write an original one to sing as you close this study, to express how you feel toward God today.

T hree dogs live at my house. My son owns a huge male Chesapeake Bay retriever. My daughter has an eight-pound sheltie. In between is a chocolate lab, Wafer Thin Mint, my dog. She deserves honorable mention in this book for two reasons. She helped to write it by nudging a ball into my lap every time the noise of my computer printer signaled a switch in my concentration. But more important, she exemplifies in her canine way something of the kind of attitude we have been considering throughout this study.

Wafer is fixated on the concept "ball." She is neither the fastest nor the strongest of the three dogs, but she almost always comes up with it in any game of catch or hide-and-seek, even though a car accident crippled her left hind leg when she was a puppy. She risks everything, crashing into walls or bushes, diving into water or under furniture, outmaneuvering the other two dogs, and hanging on with one purpose: to be the one to put that ball—that muddy, slobbery treasure—into my hand. She has invented and perfected numerous versions of rolling the ball with her nose to a human player—up or down stairs, across carpets or smooth floors, through tunnels.

It isn't so much the ball itself Wafer loves. She doesn't lie around and gnaw on it by the hour, and she makes no protest when Frango or Roca pick it up for a chew or two. Any of several balls will do, and a hefty new stick picked up in the woods is just as much fun. For Wafer, the joy is in the *relationship* expressed in all the games we play. When I throw a ball, she is determined to bring it back at any cost. When she deposits it in my hand or shoves it into my thigh, she wholeheartedly expects that I will throw it again. And again, and again. Only a dog lover can appreciate how clearly she manifests her sense of betrayal if I refuse to respond or if I tease her by letting one of the other dogs take it away. In a few minutes, however, they have lost interest, and she is happily back again with a new invitation to play.

God wants you to be fixated on him—not merely obsessed with the concept of Christianity and its objective manifestations, but focused intently on your personal, "ongrowing" relationship with your creator and redeemer, the one who calls you by name and responds to your cry as his unique, beloved child.

> Therefore, holy brothers, who share in the heavenly calling, fix your thoughts on Jesus, the apostle and high priest whom we confess. He was faithful to the one who appointed him, just as Moses was faithful in all God's house. Jesus has been found worthy of greater honor than Moses, just as the builder of a house has greater honor than the house itself. For every house is built by someone, but God is the builder of everything. Moses was faithful as a servant in all God's house, testifying to what would be said in the future. But Christ is faithful as a son over God's house. And we are his house, if we hold on to our courage

169

and the hope of which we boast (Heb. 3:1–6; see also Heb. 12:1–3).

> Therefore we do not lose heart. Though outwardly we are wasting away, yet inwardly we are being renewed day by day. For our light and momentary troubles are achieving for us an eternal glory that far outweighs them all. So we fix our eyes not on what is seen, but on what is unseen. For what is seen is temporary, but what is unseen is eternal (2 Cor. 4:16–18).

After God gave Israel the second set of stone tablets on which were inscribed the Ten Commandments, he wanted to be sure they remembered and obeyed them, to receive his blessing and not a curse:

> Fix these words of mine in your hearts and minds; tie them as symbols on your hands and bind them on your foreheads. Teach them to your children, talking about them when you sit at home and when you walk along the road, when you lie down and when you get up. Write them on the doorframes of your houses and on your gates, so that your days and the days of your children may be many in the land that the LORD swore to give your forefathers, as many as the days that the heavens are above the earth (Deut. 11:18–21).

God wants us to be certain in our minds about his constancy; even when we have rejected him, he continues to work out his plans:

> "Remember this, fix it in mind, take it to heart, you rebels.
> Remember the former things, those of long ago;
>> I am God, and there is no other;
>> I am God, and there is none like me.
> I make known the end from the beginning,
>> from ancient times, what is still to come.
> I say: My purpose will stand, and I will do all that I please" (Isa. 46:8–10; see also Amos 9:4).

Likewise, God has fixed his eye on his people for our good, and we can rest assured of his constant "watchcare" over us: "For the eyes of the LORD range throughout the earth to strengthen those whose hearts are fully committed to him" (2 Chron. 16:9).

> I lift up my eyes to the hills—
>   where does my help come from?
> My help comes from the LORD,
>   the Maker of heaven and earth.
>
> He will not let your foot slip—
>   he who watches over you will not slumber;
> indeed, he who watches over Israel
>   will neither slumber nor sleep.
>
> The LORD watches over you—
>   the LORD is your shade at your right hand;
> the sun will not harm you by day,
>   nor the moon by night.
>
> The LORD will keep you from all harm—
>   he will watch over your life;
> the LORD will watch over your coming and going
>   both now and forevermore.   (Ps. 121)

I hope you have begun to realize that our focus in this book has *not* actually been on a particular phrase or a consistent pattern of response, after all. Even as we have identified *Henani* as a unifying theme, the attitudes and actions of each of the central characters have been unique. God, knowing their special strengths and their deepest needs, invited each one into an intimate relationship with himself, and they answered, "Yes, Lord" with their lives, each in his own way.

Scan the contents page and your summary of each of the men whose lives we have examined. Although I tried to come up with a key word or phrase to develop a particular point I wanted to make about their personalities, it has not been my intention to persuade you that my ideas are the only ones possible. That is why I offered you the format of studying the questions first by yourself with your Bible. If you never discussed your answers in a group or read my chapter afterward, you still would have achieved my primary goal, which is to invite you to "taste and see that the Lord is good" (Ps. 34:8), by digging deeply into his word. Only there can you begin to know God by his voice, so that you can respond more fully when he calls.

Now, it is not so much a matter of determining which of the ten biblical personalities most resembles our own so that we can model our behavior accordingly, although we do want to be wise in applying the lessons of Scripture to ourselves for our edification and encouragement. While it is fascinating to see in how many ways God has dealt with individuals in the past, it is even more exciting to realize that he desires to have a unique relationship with each one of us today.

Even as I learned something valuable by considering these characters from a particular perspective, I learned even more about the character of God in his dealings with each one. I realized that the chapter subtitles could serve a dual purpose: as clues to the human personalities as well as an opportunity to magnify the Lord as I gained new appreciation for his attributes. Starting with Adam's sense of shame, which kept him from stepping out of the bushes when God called him, I remembered the *shame* that Christ, our second Adam, endured for our sakes on the cross. God *sacrificed* his only begotten son, whom he loved even more than Abraham loved Isaac, whom he spared (John 3:16). Though we, like Isaac, often think of ourselves and our desires first and ignore God's promises, he is *sovereign* in working out all things according to his perfect purposes, either with our help or in spite of our *selfishness*.

Jacob seemed to have to learn the hard way that there is no *security* in self; but in God we may rest in the knowledge that we have eternal life, that no one can snatch us out of his hand (John 10:28). Just as Joseph provided a model of human service, he is sometimes considered to be a type of Christ, the perfect *servant*, the branch through whom God removed "the sin of this land in a single day" (Zech. 3:8,9). Moses' sense of *smallness* reflected Christ's emptying of himself for us (Phil. 2) and was a lesson in

172

the dignity of true humility (Mark 9:35; 10:31, 44). Christ certainly is *sensitive* to us when we cry for help.

Can you finish the list, identifying events or passages in the Scriptures that speak of Jesus' *submissiveness*, the *sealing of the Spirit*, the *simplicity* of his obedience, and the *sovereignty* of God so magnificently manifest throughout the whole Bible? What else have you learned about the Lord through this study? Has he become your Lord, and have you committed yourself to be his child by faith?

Sometimes fervent Christians are overwhelmed with a sense of personal guilt, recognizing that God's only son had to die for our sins, that "I myself" nailed him to the cross. We ought with awe to contemplate the fact that for our sins alone, Jesus was willing to put his life on the line so that we might enjoy full forgiveness and have eternal life with him: "He died for me." The cross was not for our punishment, but for our salvation. It was the only way to restore the fellowship between God and his people broken by Adam in Eden when he opted not to obey. And it was and is the sufficient way through which we can come freely into his presence daily and forever.

Perhaps it is still not perfectly clear to what place or purpose God has called you, or what specific project he has designed just for you. But I trust that you have become more aware that what God desires is a continuing *relationship* with you—that no matter where you are, you are with him. So, while we have examined in detail these ten lives, and you have peeked into one another's lives if you have shared this study with a group, the only life that really matters is yours. What have you learned about your own character, and about God's ways of working in the world, inviting individuals into his service, offering numerous opportunities to be his partners in the fulfilling of his purposes, which *will* be accomplished? We return to the same questions we asked at the beginning: Who are you? Where are you? How are you responding to God's call?

May the mind of Christ my Saviour
Live in me from day to day,
By his love and power controlling
All I do and say.

May the Word of God dwell richly
In my heart from hour to hour,
So that all may see I triumph
Only through His power,

May the peace of God, my Father,
Rule my life in everything,
That I may be calm to comfort
Sick and sorrowing.

May the love of Jesus fill me
As the waters fill the sea;
Him exalting, self abasing,
This is victory.

May I run the race before me,
Strong and brave to face the foe,
Looking only unto Jesus
As I onward go.

May His beauty rest upon me
As I seek the lost to win,
And may they forget the channel,
Seeing only Him. Amen.

Kate B. Wilkinson, 1925